"Dr. Cheydleur takes the mystery out of effective biblical counseling. Each chapter of this helpful book will bring you closer to becoming the healing instrument God has called you to be."
LES PARROTT III, PH.D.
Seattle Pacific University
Author of *Counseling and Psychotherapy* (McGraw-Hill)

"Dr. Cheydleur brings a great deal of experience to the counseling process. His deep commitment to the Christian faith is also evident in the book. The result is a faith-based model of counseling that gently and appropriately weds biblical truths and counseling theory, which Christian counselors will find helpful."
LAWRENCE E. RESSLER, PH.D., ACSW
President, North American Association of Christians in Social Work

"We need skills training. I wish that I had been helped through the lessons in this book at an earlier point in my ministry and medical practice. The author has included useful resources rather than arcane references and has documented every point with down-to-earth, easy-to-relate-to examples from his own unusually broad clinical experience."
HERBERT C. RADER, M.D., FACS
Vice President of Clinical Affairs, New York Presbyterian Healthcare Network
Medical Advisor, The Salvation Army, Eastern USA

"I would highly recommend this book to anyone who is seeking to do counseling, or for counselors who are looking to improve their skills."
THOMAS WHITEMAN, PH.D.
Founder and President, Life Counseling Services

# CALLED to COUNSEL

COUNSELING SKILLS HANDBOOK

# CALLED
## — to —
# COUNSEL

### John R. Cheydleur, Ph.D., ACSW

Tyndale House Publishers, Inc.
Wheaton, Illinois

For further information, contact
  Captain/Dr. John Cheydleur
  Phone: (914) 620-7383
  Fax: (914) 620-7759
  E-mail: jcheydleur@use.salvationarmy.org

Visit Tyndale s exciting Web site at www.tyndale.com

Designed by Julie Chen

Published in association with The Salvation Army

Includes bibliographical references

**Library of Congress Cataloging-in-Publication Data**

Cheydleur, John R.
  Called to counsel : counseling skills handbook / John R. Cheydleur.
    p.  cm.
  Includes bibliographical references.
  ISBN 0-8423-3243-X (alk. paper)
  1. Pastoral counseling Handbooks, manuals, etc.    I. Title
BV4012.2.C445 1999
253.5 dc21                                            99-051873

Printed in the United States of America

06  05  04  03  02  01  00
9   8   7   6   5   4   3   2   1

The first thing is to acquire wisdom;

gain understanding though it cost you all you have.

Do not forsake her, and she will keep you safe;

love her, and she will guard you;

cherish her, and she will lift you high;

if only you embrace her, she will bring you to honour.

She will set a garland of grace on your head

and bestow on you a crown of glory.

Proverbs 4:7-10, NEB

# THE FAITH-BASED COUNSELING PROCESS

**Client Feels Instability**
Isolation, weakness, aloneness, confused thinking, contradictory behavior, unbelief, unrealistic belief

**Request for Counseling**
Counselor is sensitive to the opportunity for brief counseling

**Reflection of Content**
Counselor helps client to become accurate and specific about facts, sequences, etc.

**Empathizing with Feelings**
Counselor helps client to accept and express feelings

**Mirroring Values**
Counselor helps client to see connection between values, value conflicts, feelings, and content

**Sorting Values**
Counselor helps client to identify sources of values: personal, family, cultural

**Value Comparison**
Counselor helps client compare prior values to biblical values/standards

**Value Choice**
Client chooses value(s) on which to base decisions

**Connecting Feelings to Values**
Counselor helps client to examine feelings about values

**Decision Making**
Client makes new decision(s) based on clear values and accurate facts

**Action Planning**
Client and counselor brainstorm and evaluate new possibilities to create a specific action plan

**Client Achieves Stability**
Accountability to group/individual, strength/support, clear thinking, focused behavior, sane spirituality

**Forward Progress in Counseling**

Note: At each level, the interview may go to a deeper level of problem/opportunity exploration or may move across to a same-level solution step.

Level of Counseling Depth

# THANK YOU

To Judy Cheydleur and Andrew Cheydleur

To Lenore Lass and Amy MacLean

To Colonel W. Todd Bassett and Major Midge Wheeler of The Salvation Army

To Petra DeCaille-Poleon

To Doug Elliott and Tammy Faxel of Tyndale House

To Keith Miller, Dr. Howard Clinebell, and Ed Forster

To all the students who have contributed so much to this book

# Doc & Duck

# Table of Contents

Foreword     xvii

The Story behind This Book     xix

Self-Paced Skills Training     xxiii


## BASIC SKILLS

Chapter One **Basic Counseling Mistakes**     3

The first rule of counseling is to do no harm. Learn to avoid the twelve most common counseling mistakes.

Back Talk     24

Taped Interview Analysis     25

The Counselor's Library     27

Chapter Two **Basic Interview Structure**     29

Christian workers often counsel in unstructured settings. Learn how to set up a brief, effective interview.

Back Talk     52

Taped Interview Analysis     53

The Counselor's Library     55

Chapter Three **Basic Listening Skills**     57

Active listening is more than being quiet. Listen to God, yourself, and your client. Learn to reflect content, emotion, and values.

Back Talk     74

Taped Interview Analysis     75

The Counselor's Library     76


## ADVANCED SKILLS

Chapter Four **Advanced Listening Skills**     79

The experienced counselor goes beyond support and acceptance. Learn to help your client reconnect content and emotion with key values.

Back Talk     90

Taped Interview Analysis     91

The Counselor's Library     93

Chapter Five **Advanced Challenging Skills**     95

Listening and reflection are not the only tools in the counselor's toolkit. Learn to use probes and prompts to move your interview to a deeper level.

Give-and-Take Interview Review 107

Back Talk 108

Taped Interview Analysis 109

The Counselor's Library 111

Chapter Six Advanced Action-Planning Skills 113
Counseling results in actions that change circumstances. Move from counselor to coach as your client
develops and tests new action plans.

Back Talk 137

Taped Interview Analysis 138

The Counselor's Library 140

## SPECIALTY SKILLS

Chapter Seven Specialty Scripture Skills 143
Counseling is different from preaching. Learn to
provide confidence to your client by presenting
Scripture as new and welcome information.

Back Talk 163

Taped Interview Analysis 163

The Counselor's Library 165

Chapter Eight Specialty Prayer Skills 167
Prayer can be used or misused in counseling. Learn to
help your client develop a realistic faith in what God
can do.

Back Talk 184

Taped Interview Analysis 185

The Counselor's Library 187

Chapter Nine Specialty Intervention Skills 189
Some clients don't believe in demons; others attribute
many things to them. Learn how to help your client
deal with the challenges of evil.

Back Talk 206

Taped Interview Analysis 207

The Counselor's Library 208

# CONTINUING EDUCATION

Continuing Education 101 **Written Case Notes** 211
If you counsel often, you may want to keep written
case notes. Learn the "DAP" and "SOAP" recording
systems.

Continuing Education 102 **Scripture-Based Values** 217
Many Christian counselors do not know how to apply
Scripture to clients' questions about values. Investigate
Scripture passages in four key value areas.

Continuing Education 103 **Topical Scripture References** 221
It can be difficult to quickly locate a Scripture passage
for a specific need. Use this guide to find one hundred
topical Scripture passages.

Skill Builders Index 225

Encouragement for Your Future 227

Author Information 229

# Foreword

For persons seeking to increase their competence as counselors, Dr. Cheydleur's skills-training manual, *Called to Counsel,* has many strengths:

- The steps presented in the process of counseling are clear and helpful, moving from discussing content to emotions to values and value conflicts, then to reconceptualizing decisions as a basis for developing active plans that build new actions into the client's life.
- The concrete guidelines throughout the manual are helpful, as are the illustrative cases. These are reality-based in that they include both cases in which counseling was successful and those in which, for various reasons, it was not.
- The abundance of relevant biblical passages (on almost every page) keeps the book Scripture rooted for those approaching the counseling process from a faith-based perspective. Biblical passages are integrated with useful ideas from psychology and counseling literature.
- Particularly beneficial for improving counseling skills are the discussions of how to use probes and prompts to define problems and clarify value conflicts (chapter 5) and the basic process of spiritual counseling (chapter 7).
- Dr. Cheydleur's on-target description of the ultimate purpose of counseling reflects the long heritage of The Salvation Army. It does so by recognizing social factors in understanding the complex roots of human brokenness. He states the purpose as "to restore strength to the person who is weak or stumbling and/or suffering from social oppression and brokenness."

*Called to Counsel* is a valuable book from which to learn the essential skills of this much-needed healing ministry in the broken and birthing world of the twenty-first century!

HOWARD CLINEBELL, PH.D.
Professor Emeritus, Pastoral Psychology and Counseling
Claremont School of Theology
Claremont, California, USA

# The Story behind This Book

*"If you want to see a miracle, go where there is a need." If it's true that miracles occur in areas of greatest need, I should have been seeing many miracles in the little town of Massena, New York, on the St. Lawrence Seaway in 1968, for I faced many counseling needs: a grieving widow whose husband had died in an explosion, a young professional man caught up in despair over his own adultery, and a host of referrals from church pastors who had even less background in counseling than I. But I saw no miracles.*

*I knew God was calling me to a ministry of counseling, but I was confronted daily with my lack of the skills necessary to be an effective Christian counselor.*

OF COURSE, in one sense, we are all called to counsel, whether we are cabdrivers or schoolteachers, clergy or family therapists, beauticians or social workers, recovery sponsors or best friends; we all have opportunities and obligations to give guidance and wise counsel to other people.

I had taken a perceptual psychology course as an undergraduate at Swarthmore College and a learning-theory course at Temple University. The Salvation Army School for Officer Training had provided excellent Bible courses and well-taught courses in child and adult development. But none of my classes had taught me the specific counseling skills I now needed.

I started taking seminars at Potsdam State College and enrolled in a graduate psychology class at St. Lawrence University. I signed up for the Pastoral Psychology Book Club and tried to do what the books taught. I wanted to help people in the best way possible, but I often did not know whether I was helping or hurting.

I had a sense that my Bible courses held the right answers and that my psychology courses posed the right questions, but it was often difficult to match the psychological questions and biblical answers with the human needs of the hurting people whom I was trying to help.

At that point I would have been very grateful for a simple counseling-skills book, with limited theory of any type, that would teach me to use basic counseling skills and show me when and how to use Scripture and prayer in ways that helped people and didn't offend them.

I didn't find that book. I did find an unusual theory book that pointed me in the right direction. The book I found was *The Crisis in Psychiatry and Religion* by O. Hobart Mowrer, a past president of the American Psychologial Association.

As I turned the pages and absorbed the thinking of this great man, I formed one solid belief that has undergirded my counseling ministry for more than twenty-five years: the skills of good counseling and the truths of Scripture are necessary complements of one another.

Later I learned that Dr. Mowrer had suffered from periodic bouts of depression with limited relief; out of his personal experience, he had founded Integrity Therapy, a secular psychological system modeled after the Saturday meetings of the early Methodist church, to provide a context for growth in honesty, involvement, and accountability.

At about the same time that I discovered Dr. Mowrer's book, two men were studying under him who would dramatically change the face of both pastoral counseling and professional clinical psychology. These men were Jay Adams and Gerard Egan.

Adams, an evangelical theologian, went on to write *Competent to Counsel* in 1970, a wonderful book of Christian polemic that uses the Bible as the basis for an Integrity-Therapy type of system called Nouthetic Counseling. He challenged pastors not to throw away the use of Scripture in favor of the Freudian teachings that were in vogue in much of clinical pastoral education at that time. *Competent to Counsel* is now a standard text in many seminary counseling courses.

Egan, an ordained Catholic priest and former high-school language teacher, began doing research on which verbal counseling skills were most effective in bringing about attitude and behavioral change. I had the privilege of being his graduate assistant at Loyola University of Chicago in 1970–1971 as he was field-testing the first edition of *The Skilled Helper*, a non-Freudian, research-based guide to professional counseling skills, which has become a leading text in modern graduate schools of psychology.

(Subsequently, the American Psychiatric Association revised its prestigious *Diagnostic and Statistical Manual* to eliminate many of the old tautological Freudian terms, replacing them with more accurate behavioral descriptions. Still later, changes honoring the value of religious and cultural traditions in personal growth and positive change were added.)

The book you hold in your hand, *Called to Counsel,* is in a way a "daughter" book to both *Competent to Counsel* and *The Skilled Helper.*

The philosophy of *Called to Counsel* is descended from Jay Adams's position that the Old and New Testaments provide sufficient guidance and instruction for Christian living, without the introduction of non-Christian theories and philosophies, to create a healthy personal worldview.

The practice of *Called to Counsel* is descended from Gerard Egan's position that research can identify a body of practical, learnable skills that create positive counseling outcomes.

The position of *Called to Counsel* is that you can learn specific counseling skills, which are not mysterious; these skills do not have to be tied to specific psychological or social theories, and they are most effective when used in conjunction with the sensitive application of scriptural truths.

In a very real sense, *Called to Counsel* is the "granddaughter" book of *The Crisis in Psychiatry and Religion* and seeks, like many human grandchildren, to be the practical outworking of the ideals of its heritage.

*Called to Counsel* will teach you very little theory of any type. Instead, it seeks to be the book for which I was searching back in Massena, New York. It trains you to use eleven basic counseling skills and provides dozens of practical tips and advanced techniques to make your counseling more effective.

For me, the heart of *Called to Counsel* is contained in those sections that clearly demonstrate the use and misuse of prayer in counseling and that show you how and when to introduce Scripture as a source of new information for value sorting and decision making.

Finally, *Called to Counsel* shows you how to move from the dependency-maintaining role of counselor to the independence-creating role of action-planning coach—it teaches you to help people help themselves.

I have a vivid memory of my visit to the University of Illinois, Champaign-Urbana campus, to meet O. Hobart Mowrer. I remember being shown to his faculty office—cluttered with shelves and files of research and dominated by a huge old rolltop desk—and waiting for this grand old man to arrive.

He was surprisingly small, wearing a brown cardigan sweater. I thought he might be the janitor. Then he introduced himself and shared his life and ideas, and he grew to fill the room. I told him of an ambition—to build a life and ministry in which counseling skills and scriptural values would be married to each other in a unified whole—and I received his encouragement.

It has been more than twenty-five years since that visit, and I have had many opportunities to grow as a Christian counselor. Before I became ready to write *Called to Counsel,* I served as a Salvation Army officer, a family-services director, the director of a Christian psychiatric center, a graduate-school professor, the president of Trinity College of Graduate Studies, and then back with The Salvation Army as a counselor trainer and social-services consultant.

I think that Dr. Mowrer would be pleased with this book.

Skim the first chapter of *Called to Counsel* rapidly to remind yourself of some of the common counseling mistakes and to acquaint yourself with the basic skills you will be developing to avoid those mistakes. As you read, allow yourself to review the hope that is possible through the everyday miracles of Christian counseling. Then set aside three hours a week for nine weeks. Study one chapter each week, spending one hour on the text and two hours completing the suggested action items and training exercises. Your twenty-seven-hour investment will return to you in many ways.

Don't be surprised if some common counseling needs turn into everyday miracles!

JOHN R. CHEYDLEUR, PH.D., ACSW
West Nyack, New York

# Self-Paced Skills Training

ALL OF US are "called to counsel" in some way. Some of us are simply neighbors, friends, parents, or adult children with responsibilities for others. Some of us are pastors and teachers or Christian social workers. Some are nurses or recovery sponsors. All of us want to give the very best help we can.

You may have been introduced to this book through a college course or continuing-education seminar. You may have purchased it as an individual. The *Called to Counsel* skills-training manual may be used in many ways to improve your counseling skills.

Here is one plan for using this manual as a self-paced individual training program: During the first hour, read one of the skills-building chapters, and make notes to yourself in the margin or in a separate notebook. Then complete the "Back Talk" page at the end of the chapter. Stop at the end of the first hour whether you have completed all of the reading and feedback or not.

During the second hour, fill in the "Skill Builder" exercises throughout the chapter you have just read. Stop at the end of the second hour whether you have completed all of the exercises or not.

During the third hour, conduct and tape-record a practice counseling interview. Ask a friend, another student, or a family member to work with you on this exercise. Ask him or her to talk about something real (not role-play!). The topic may be happy or sad, important or merely trivial, so long as it is real! The person should talk, and you should practice responding. Use the counseling techniques and principles highlighted in the chapter. Do this for twenty or thirty minutes with your tape recorder running. Then spend a half hour playing the tape back. Complete the "Taped Interview Analysis" form that appears at the end of the chapter.

Stop this exercise at the end of the third hour.

Repeat the above sequence for each of the nine chapters in this book. Practice your new counseling skills from each chapter, and reemphasize the skills you have already learned from prior chapters. You can learn the specific techniques of faith-based counseling in just twenty-seven hours of intensive, structured study and experience.

## Expanded Resources Are Available

Each chapter concludes with "The Counselor's Library," a focused selection of expanded resources. These will provide helpful additional information about the specific faith-based counseling skills and principles covered in the chapter. Each resource listing includes one or more key books to expand your biblical knowledge and to increase your understanding of human behavior.

## Our Most Significant Resource

Of course, the most significant resource we bring into our personal counseling is our grateful experience of spiritual acceptance by God. This enables us to respond to Him and to be Spirit-led by Him (2 Cor. 1:4). The faith-based counseling skills you learn will be helpful in focusing the way you draw on your experience with God. However, they are not substitutes for personal spiritual experiences. It is only through the leading of the Holy Spirit that you will be able to select the appropriate skills, resources, and/or responses to use in each situation.

## Your Skills-Development Baseline

Before you actually begin this skills-training program, briefly write out your answers to the following three questions. This will provide a baseline to which you can refer as you watch your skills develop.

1. What personal counseling skills do I already know how to use? _____

_____

_____

_____

2. What spiritual counseling skills would I like to improve? _____

_____

_____

_____

3. What areas of faith-based counseling would I like to learn more about? __

_____

_____

_____

Christian psychiatrist David B. Larson, M.D., MSPH, has given us this challenge: "As people committed both to Jesus Christ and to the effective care of individuals, we can demonstrate to other professionals that we are worth our salt and that Christian counselors stand in the front ranks of competent helpers for people in need."

Turn the page to begin to make this challenge come true!

# PART ONE

# BASIC SKILLS

Doc & Duck © 1999 Andrew J. Cheydleur

# Basic Counseling Mistakes

THERE ARE twelve common counseling mistakes. As you learn to identify and avoid each of these mistakes, you will find that you are also learning the basic building blocks of the counseling process. Each basic skill area is outlined below, along with the common mistakes that the development of this skill will help you avoid.

The book of Proverbs affirms the value of good counseling: "A word fitly spoken is like apples of gold in settings of silver. Like an earring of gold and an ornament of fine gold is a wise rebuker to an obedient ear" (Proverbs 25:11-12). However, the same picturesque passage reminds us that misplaced confidence, in a time of trouble, "is like a bad tooth and a foot out of joint" (Prov. 25:19).

## Mistake Number One: Patronizing or Cliché Responses

*Several years ago a counselor began to see a depressed, divorced woman. Helen's church had not provided any emotional support to her after her husband ran off with his secretary. The key mistake that members of her church had made was to use patronizing responses. They were attempting to control and limit her grief and anger at being abandoned. Some people had asked her to look into her own heart and see what she had done to contribute to the divorce. Others had told her that she would "get over it." Some had used clichés or jargon responses such as "time heals all wounds" or "God still has a plan for your life."*

It is very easy for us to minimize another person's pain or confusion, because others' pain may call up our own unhealed wounds. To avoid this mistake, the church people would have had to listen to the woman at a deep, caring level. At the same time, it is important that we who are believers be "kind to one another, tenderhearted, forgiving one another, even as God in Christ forgave [us]" (Ephesians 4:32). We show that we care by reflecting not only the content but the emotion with which the person is struggling. In order to do this well, we have to keep ourselves open enough to hear the emotion and not be frightened by it.

*To repair this mistake, it took about eight weeks of once-a-week counseling, focusing primarily on deep listening, reflection, and empathy. Eventually, Helen was able to formulate an action plan to put some happiness and joy back into her life. She planned a two-week vacation with her children and her sister. They traveled by motor home, visiting a number of interesting places she had always wanted to see! The trip proved to be very helpful for her and for the whole family. The action plan could not have developed in a meaningful way without the concentration on empathy and a refusal on the counselor's part to avoid her pain by employing patronizing or jargon responses.*

**Skill Builder 1.1** As you complete the Skill Builder exercises in this chapter, look for the common mistakes and errors in counseling. Also, be sensitive to the ways in which basic counseling skills are positively demonstrated. Look at each example of client statements and counselor responses. Mark each response either "correct" or "mistake," and tell why. Then write a correct response of your own.

*Client:* "I am so frustrated! I don't want to be a bishop's wife, playing all those religious politics! I like being the wife of an Episcopal priest in a small town, but they want him to be a bishop! Help!"

*Counselor:* "Well, maybe your being a bishop's wife could be a good thing for both of you. Besides, your husband really would be a good bishop."

Correct ❏          Mistake ❏

Why? _____

Write your own caring response: _____

_____

_____

_____

See chapter 2 for basic empathy skills and healthy ways to deal with question traps and "ain't-it-awful" lists.

Chapter 4 provides additional information on reconnecting content, emotions, and values as preparation for decision making and action planning.

## Mistake Number Two: Questions and Probes Too Soon

*When I was beginning in the ministry, I served one summer as a cadet (intern) at The Salvation Army Corps in Pottsville, Pennsylvania. One morning a mildly mentally retarded forty-year-old man came into my office. He asked if he could afford to move to his own apartment and stop living with his mother.*

*I made the mistake of focusing only on the topic of finance. I used many questions and probes to explore his financial situation. I helped him write up an elaborate budget, which, unfortunately, proved that he would not be able to afford to live on his own. At the end of this lengthy hour-and-a-half session, he thanked me profusely for my time. He shook my hand before leaving the building.*

*Later, as I left to go to lunch, I found his carefully drawn-up budget torn into a thousand pieces and scattered all over our front sidewalk! My premature sense was that this issue was all about finances. That had led me to use a number of probes and questions that kept the entire interview focused in that area. I neglected the extreme emotional pain that he was suffering from living with his tyrannical, emotionally abusive mother!*

Questions and probes, such as "When did this happen?"; "Tell me a little more about it"; and "Can you give me an example?" can be very helpful in

moving an interview along, especially if it seems to have stalled and the client doesn't know how to proceed. However, one of the most common mistakes for inexperienced spiritual counselors is the use of questions or other strong probes too soon in the interview. This may put the counselor in the position of "leading" the interview and focusing it too narrowly on a particular topic before the emotional, spiritual, and social dynamics have been adequately explored.

One reason this may happen is that the counselor is trying to avoid hearing the client's pain. Another may be that the person being counseled has produced some information that has attracted the counselor's attention and interest but is really a sidetrack to the primary, yet-unexpressed need.

To repair an interview that is on a sidetrack, it must be "backed up" to a relationship- and empathy-building stage.

Probes and questions are most useful during the period of an interview or interview series when information must be gathered to form an adequate action plan. However, if they are used prematurely, the action plan that is formulated may ignore critical social, emotional, or spiritual areas of the client's life. You may actually prevent your client from discussing these areas by inappropriately narrowing the focus of the interview.

---

### ☝ **Skill Builder 1.2**

*Client:* "Well, that about wraps it up; I think you've given me all the tools I need to move out of the rehabilitation center and resume a normal life."

*Counselor:* "Could you give me an example of one of those 'tools' and just how you see it working for you on the outside?"

Correct ❑          Mistake ❑

Why? _____
_____
_____

Write your own careful "probe" or question: _____
_____
_____
_____

---

See chapter 5 for additional information on using prompts, probes, and questions in a timely and effective way.

## Mistake Number Three: Inappropriate Self-Disclosure

*One of my graduate students had an unusual experience during her practicum at a community mental-health agency. She was able to build rapport with a regressed, mentally retarded older woman. The woman seemed to withdraw into herself and would not communicate with any other therapists at the agency.*

*Why did the student therapist succeed where the more experienced therapists had failed with this woman? She succeeded because she shared with the client (privately) her own fears at going into therapy some years earlier. She also shared some of her own fears of eventually being a successful therapist. This made it "OK" for the woman to open up to her.*

*The client shared her fears of being manipulated by therapists and the mental health system, as had previously happened to her in contacts with other official agencies. Of course, it also helped when they discovered each other as believers in Jesus Christ who valued their own personal prayer lives but had very few people with whom they could share spiritual matters.*

*Selective, focused self-disclosure on the part of the counselor often unblocks difficult areas for the client. Today my former graduate student is a highly regarded child psychologist who continues to use focused self-disclosure to reach some of her most difficult young clients.*

The appropriate use of self-disclosure can build a stronger bond between the counselor and client, help to break down the client's sense of isolation, and provide a very real hope. However, one of the most common mistakes is for self-disclosure to occur too early in the interview. Counselor self-disclosure may seem to trivialize the concerns of the client or put the counselor on a pedestal, as in, "I got through this kind of problem; why can't you?"

First, it is important that our self-sharing not assume the form of a "war story," in which the details of our life, which we think are so interesting, take up more time than we spend in supporting the client. Second, counselor self-disclosure usually should not focus on areas of the counselor's life that are still unhealed. This may invite the interview to "change roles," asking the client to become the emotional buffer and spiritual support for the person who is supposed to be the counselor! This kind of emotional flip-flop puts tremendous stress on a client who is already overloaded with his or her own unfinished business. Third, even if the inter-

view is about positive things and the counselor's self-disclosure is about something positive, it should not be done to elicit the admiration of the client. Self-disclosure should be used briefly and only to promote bonding and understanding.

In Matthew 3:1-17, Jesus came from Galilee to be baptized by John the Baptist in the Jordan River. A close reading shows how careful Jesus was to preserve a sense of respect for John's ministry and not do anything that would overshadow John or trivialize what he was doing. Similarly, we need to be very careful in revealing our own material so that we do not overwhelm the client, and we need to keep the focus of the interview on the needs of the client.

### 👋 Skill Builder 1.3

*Client:* "You know how mad I was a few weeks ago when my girlfriend went to bed with another guy? I think part of that was I'm afraid I might not be man enough for her. I mean, you know, sometimes I think I might be attracted to another man instead of a woman."

*Counselor:* "Well, I wouldn't let it worry you too much. I never told anybody else this, but when I was twelve, I had a same-sex friend named Sandy that I was kind of attracted to, but he moved away, and I got over it."

Correct ❏           Mistake ❏

Why? _____

_____

Write your own appropriate self-disclosure: _____

_____

_____

_____

To avoid mistakes in using self-disclosure in counseling, follow these four principles:

1. Do it for the client's need, not your own.
2. Keep your sharing brief, then move right back to what the client feels and thinks.
3. Listen to the client's spirit and the Holy Spirit, not just your own spirit.
4. When you share, don't seek to have the client respond to your feelings.

To repair a mistake of too-early or too-intense self-disclosure, ask the client how he or she felt when you were talking. Reflect the feelings and content of the client's answer nondefensively, then shift the focus back to the client.

All use of self-disclosure should be focused to promote the purpose of the counseling interview, as described in chapter 3.

## Mistake Number Four: Advice instead of Information

*While my wife and I were Salvation Army officers in East Orange, New Jersey, we started a twenty-four-hour crisis telephone hot line. One of our crisis telephone staff members had not completed her college education. Previously she had worked for several group homes and in other social-work settings. At the same time, she attended three or four different colleges. She was not able to get them to accept each other's credits to assist her toward the goal of completing her bachelor's degree.*

*Telling her that she needed to go back to college would have been simply "giving advice." It would have increased her frustration and sense of failure. Instead, I listened as she explored not only the kind of education she had obtained but the way she was planning to finish school.*

*When she finished speaking, I was able to tell her about Thomas Edison College, an accredited member of the New Jersey State College system. This college assembles transcripts and evaluates prior learning experiences toward degree completion. I supplied her with the appropriate information only after determining that she had the motivation to follow through with it.*

*She later submitted all her transcripts to Thomas Edison, as well as some of her life-experience learning. She found that she was only two courses short of a bachelor's degree! She took those courses locally and went on to enter Columbia University's School of Social Work to work on her MSW.*

One of the major mistakes commonly made by new counselors is to confuse the necessary process of introducing new information to the client with the negative process of giving advice.

Scripture tells us that a wise reproof that finds "attentive ears" is better than the most beautiful gold jewelry (Proverbs 25:12, NEB). Notice that there are two parts to the concept. To be a wise reprover, or advice giver, has no value unless there is receptiveness on the part of the receiver. As a spiritual counselor, it is your responsibility to gauge the receptivity of the client—and/or help the client become receptive—before new information is imparted. It is a cop-out for you to say, "I gave the right advice, but the client didn't take it."

The process of introducing new information requires that the counselor first explore the issues involved with the client. Then the counselor must care deeply about the client's concerns. Third, the counselor may supply specific information that the client does not have but needs in order to make a decision or to implement an action plan. It is important for the counselor to separate the imperative of "you should do this" from the transmission of information about "how to do this."

To avoid the "you-should" mistake in advice giving, always try to give the client two or three choices (any of which you could support) so that he or she doesn't feel boxed in.

To repair a too-strong "you-should" approach, ask clients how they felt when you were advising them, then supportively reflect their emotions. Admit there may be more than one option available. Even when the issue is clearly a moral one, there are still legitimate choices to be made about timing, style, personal or written communication, etc.

---

### ☝ Skill Builder 1.4

*Client:* "I'm very angry at my company, and especially my boss, because I don't think they're crediting my retirement account properly. I'm not saying that they are *trying* to cheat me, but even if they're not, I'm still the victim of their bad bookkeeping!"

*Counselor:* "Here's the name and number of your union representative: Samuel _____, at 831-_____."

Correct ❑          Mistake ❑

Why? _____

_____

Write your own response. _____

_____

_____

_____

---

For more detail about how to introduce any kind of new information, see the section "Scripture As Unique Information" in chapter 7.

## Mistake Number Five: Misuse or Nonuse of Scripture

*In chapter 9 you will read about Tim, who came to our clinic wearing mirrored sunglasses so that no one could see his eyes! He turned out to be a lonely, introverted, alienated individual who had no friends and almost no socialization. He took the sunglasses off at night when he was sleeping, but he wore them everywhere else, even on the job. His therapist, a very skilled and caring Chris-*

*tian clinical social worker, was able to bring him to the point where he would converse with his fellow workers. He began to talk to the counter clerks in the stores where he shopped. The therapist did not err on the side of misusing Scripture as advice or being too casual with it. However, he did not have sufficient biblical knowledge to apply Scripture appropriately. After about six weeks, the therapy reached an impasse, and progress seemed to be blocked. Although he was now speaking to other people on a superficial level, Tim still did not seem to want to engage in building any deep personal relationships.*

*With Tim's permission, a pastor was brought in to one of the therapy sessions. The pastor read two very specific Scriptures regarding fellowship in the church and the breaking of bondage. Then he prayed a short, caring prayer of deliverance.*

*During the ensuing weeks, after the application of these Scriptures and prayer, therapy began to pick up speed. Tim was able to begin to develop some personal relationships in appropriate ways. Finally, his symbolic shield against the outer world, the mirrored sunglasses, came off for the first time in many years!*

During a guest lecture at a Christian college in the Midwest, one of the psychology professors lamented that he did not feel he had an adequate foundation in Scripture. Therefore, he could not integrate the Bible with material in class or use Scripture effectively with his private-practice clients. One of the strengths a Christian counselor can bring to the client is a deep knowledge of the Bible and the ability to be led by the Spirit, using specific Scripture to meet the client's needs. Your knowledge (or lack of knowledge) of Scripture may be limiting your effectiveness as a spiritual counselor; if so, you will want to obtain one or more of the specialized references listed at the end of chapter 7 to build your skills in using the Bible in a focused fashion within the counseling process.

Scripture may be correctly used in spiritual counseling either to confirm and strengthen a client's Christian values or to confront nonbiblical values that could lead the client to make a wrong decision.

We should be bold when we speak the Word of God (Acts 4:29-31). We also need to avoid the common mistake of using Scripture as concealed advice to bolster our own position. Another mistake is to patronize, using Scripture in a clichéd way. A third mistake is to imply that we are somehow better than the person we are counseling.

To avoid the misuse of Scripture, we need to learn it well and be humble before God about our own needs and failures. One beginning counselor adopted this rule: "I only refer to Scripture that I've applied to my own life. In doing this, I've been able to apply it to the needs of the counselee without being judgmental."

To repair the mistake of using the Bible in a way that is manipulative, patronizing, or arrogant, we must first repent before God and openly apologize to the client. In this way we acknowledge that we are also sinners dependent on the mercy of God, even though our sins may be different from those of our client.

The Bible describes itself as "living and powerful, and sharper than any two-edged sword, piercing even to the division of soul and spirit" (Heb. 4:12). When used appropriately and sensitively, Scripture functions as a discerner of the thoughts and intentions of the heart, but any sharp instrument can also be used maliciously or carelessly, to the destruction of the person with whom it comes in contact.

### ⚡ Skill Builder 1.5

*Client:* "For fifteen years I have put in the extra hours and made family sacrifices because I wanted to become a vice president of this company, and I'm so close I can touch it! But now I've found out that we're involved in selling stolen Russian and American military equipment to terrorists. We're just the underwriter, mind you, but if they offer me a vice presidency next week, I will probably have to take personal responsibility for this."

*Counselor:* "Obviously, you will have to turn down the promotion. God will give you the strength to do it. Remember, the Bible tells us in James 4:7, 'Resist the devil and he will flee from you.'"

Correct ❑          Mistake ❑

Why? _____

_____

Write your own response, using Scripture to focus on values: _____

_____

_____

To be effective in counseling, Scripture must be used surgically, delicately, and sensitively. It is not used to demean or punish the client, nor is it used casually or argumentatively. Instead, the Word must be applied with power at the right time and in the right way.

See chapter 7 for additional information about using Scripture in counseling.

## Mistake Number Six: Overlooking Client Values

*Mr. Anderson, a grandfather referred to the clinic by the court, was accused of molesting his granddaughter. He denied any such involvement. After careful investigation, the police determined that he had been out of town at the time the molestation had occurred. His story was accurate. However, he seemed far more agitated than he should have been and was unable to coherently marshal his own defense.*

*The therapist attended to the values that Mr. Anderson expressed. She mirrored them back to him for affirmation or correction. In this way she was able to work below his initial level of protest against having false sexual guilt. Eventually she helped him admit that he had been an extreme pornography addict before his Christian conversion, which had occurred about ten years before this incident. His use of pornography had included child pornography. To his horror it seemed as though the sin that he had contemplated in his imagination against unnamed children was now returning to haunt him even though he presently had no such thought, desire, or action. The counselor was able to help him bring this particular area of his former thought-life to the Lord for forgiveness and healing.*

*Eventually, he became a person who could stand alongside his daughter and be a healing agent for her in her concern over the grandchild. The counselor did not stop with Mr. Anderson's emotions of shock and outrage. She caught the significance of his early expression of value, which indicated it was horrible that anyone would ever do such a thing to a child. Because she listened carefully to his deepest values, her client was sufficiently healed to become a positive part of the healing of the family.*

One of the temptations of a beginning counselor is to respond to weakly expressed or unbiblical client values by using condescending responses or judgmental remarks.

To avoid this mistake, we need to have a clear view of scriptural values coupled with true humility (not defensiveness) about our own values. Then we need to listen carefully and respectfully to the client's own values and value conflicts.

Once we get beneath the content expressed in the first presentation of the problem, we can deeply and empathetically explore the client's emotions.

Then we will begin to understand the values and beliefs that the client is trying to apply to his or her life situation. Often these values will be the first the client struggles to express. They may not be the only values the client has available to bring to bear on the decision-making process.

Many clients will already be believers at some level. Therefore, it is important for the counselor to trust the power of the client's relationship as a child of God because of the individual's belief in Jesus Christ (Gal. 3:26). It is important to respond to the client's expressed values with the same sensitivity, caring, and respect that one would with a beloved family member.

In value-mirroring, spiritually sensitive counselors go beyond reflecting content or even emotions. They hold up the client's values (good and bad) for the client to look at as if he or she were looking in a mirror. For instance: "So, Molly, for you, one of the greatest values in life is serving other people even if you get no reward for it."

### Skill Builder 1.6

*Client:* "My wife and I are expecting a new baby, and I need to get a second job, but the only one I can find is a telemarketing job that pays commission only and passes it 'under the table.'"

*Counselor:* "How much and how often will you get paid?"

Correct ❑          Mistake ❑

Why? _____

_____

Write your own response, including a restatement of what you believe to be the client's values: _____

_____

_____

_____

For additional information about moving from content to emotion to values, read the sections "Discover the Content and Emotion First" and "Clarify Values and Beliefs" in chapter 7.

## Mistake Number Seven: Misuse of Prayer

*We had a very talented couple come to the clinic for marriage counseling. He was the music minister of a very large church, and she was a gifted musician in her own right. They came seeking prayer for their marriage, which was in great danger of falling apart, since they had many different schedules, commitments, and separate ambitions.*

*A wise and sensitive counselor on our staff actually refused to pray with them during the first interview but laid out a pattern of emotions, values, and behaviors they needed to develop within the marriage and their ministry careers before he would be willing to pray. As they attended the counseling session each week to discuss their struggles and failures as well as successes and feelings of satisfaction, they began to meet the conditions for answered prayer. After six weeks, the counselor felt ready to pray for the success of their marriage, and the couple had made sufficient progress to be able to genuinely participate in that prayer.*

*Although they have had a few "check-back" visits over the years, their marriage has done extremely well, and their careers have not suffered for the new attention and intensity that they have committed to the marriage.*

The two most common misuses of prayer in counseling occur when prayer is employed as a way of "preaching" or when it is used to communicate warmth or sympathy that is actually inappropriate to the counseling process. It is not the job of the pastoral counselor to "own" the problem(s) of the client.

To avoid misusing prayer in counseling, make sure you clearly state any moral concerns you have, as well as the spiritual love you have for the client, before you begin to pray.

We should be careful in our counseling responses to communicate genuine empathy and caring without communicating a cloying sympathy or over-identification with the client. The primary purpose of prayer in counseling is not to communicate caring or to preach—the central purpose is to request and receive the intervening power of God, whether to change circumstances, forgive past sin, open up acceptance into the fellowship of believers, rebuke evil forces, heal sickness, or meet other needs.

Psalm 37:3-4 says, "Trust in the Lord, and do good; dwell in the land, and feed on His faithfulness. Delight yourself also in the Lord, and He shall give you the desires of your heart." This promise has five conditions that need to be met in counseling before prayer is actually applied:

1. Trust in the Lord.
2. Do good.
3. Dwell in the land.
4. Feed on His faithfulness.
5. Delight yourself also in the Lord.

Psalm 37:5 says, "Commit your way to the Lord, trust also in Him, and He shall bring it to pass." Here again, God precedes a promise with conditions:

1. Commit your way to the Lord.
2. Trust also in Him.

Other similar lists of scriptural promises and accompanying preparatory processes remind us that prayer in counseling cannot be done cheaply, any more than prayer in life can be effective when treated casually.

There is some temptation for counselors and clients to try to use prayer as a substitute for other skills and necessary developments in counseling. Prayer cannot substitute for trust in the Lord, for a client's choosing to read Scripture in order to understand God's faithfulness, or for a client's choosing to put his or her delight in the Lord rather than in the things of "the world, the flesh, and the devil," as the Episcopal church used to say. These movements take place within the sensitive work of counseling that goes on in a series of interviews, during which the client works out these new insights in his or her daily life. As these foundations are laid, both the expectation and the right atmosphere develop for us to encourage our clients to pray and experience God's giving them the deep desires of their hearts.

---

### Skill Builder 1.7

*Client:* "Pastor, I want you to pray that my ex and I will be remarried by June first, which is our anniversary. We have been divorced for two years, and you know it is a sin. He and I should both repent and get remarried. That's what I want you to pray for."

*Counselor:* "Dear God, bring this couple back together into holy matrimony by June first of this year, and give me the honor of performing the ceremony for them. Amen."

Correct ❑        Mistake ❑

Why? _____

_____

Write your own response: _____

_____

_____

_____

For more information about using prayer in counseling, see chapter 8.

## Mistake Number Eight: Misuse of Religious Symbols

*A teenager named Mark was arrested because he and a friend went through their high school after hours, painting satanic slogans and Nazi symbols on the walls. His stepfather "sent him" to another church, where they held up a cross and tried to exorcise a demon from him. They failed to produce any change. Since that time he has been jailed for repeated acts of violence.*

The use of religious symbols has a long history within both Jewish and Christian practice. Such symbols as oil (for blessing or healing), water (to symbolize repentance), the uplifted cross (to symbolize the redeeming power of God), and placing a hand on the Bible (to symbolize integrity) have a long history of appropriate, effective use within the context of pastoral counseling. However, religious symbols can also be misused in several ways. The most common misapplication of symbols is for the pastoral counselor to select a symbol that is meaningful to his or her own faith, background, or religious community but that does not have meaning for the client. To avoid this mistake, when it is appropriate for a symbol to be used as a channel of faith, the symbol selected should be one that fits the background, belief system, and needs of the client rather than one that is merely casually appropriated from the background of the counselor.

In addition, symbols should be reserved for significant interventions. They should not be applied in isolation or in the absence of the use of a wider group of counseling skills and interventions.

The Salvation Army is "nonsacramental" and does not use symbols in ordinary worship. However, it is instructive to note that in The Salvation Army Orders and Regulations for Officers (1960), officers are wisely instructed as follows: "When persons attach importance to oil, it can be used . . . to anoint the forehead. Where an Officer has no light on this subject or does not feel a conviction . . . some other Officer or local Officer who possesses the necessary qualifications should be requested to deal with those seeking healing in this way" (page 539). As such, The Salvation Army allows its officers to be culturally and spiritually sensitive to the religious backgrounds and convictions of those to whom they minister.

In a similar fashion, pastoral counselors who come from other faith communities and who have their own symbolic emphases need to be sensitive to any difference in the symbolic awareness of their clients. They need to make sure the symbols they employ are appropriate to the person being counseled.

The reason for failure in the use of symbols for attempted deliverance, healing, or other faith-application purposes may also lie in the lack of experience or faith on the part of the pastoral counselor or other elders who are attempting to use these symbols. James 5:15 states, "The prayer of faith will save the sick." This specifically refers to the faith of the ministering person, not the faith of the person being ministered to. Therefore, it is quite unfortunate when someone attempting to use symbols as a form of ministry—or even prayer without symbols as a form of ministry—attributes any failure to a lack of faith on the part of the client. This further burdens the client with guilt and a sense of failure that should be placed with the ineffective or inexperienced pastoral counselor.

---

### ︎ Skill Builder 1.8

*Client:* "Pastor, I don't know why, but I'm having these terrible nightmares again, just like I did when I was a child. When I was ten years old, my mother took me to our minister, who dipped his finger in olive oil and made a little cross on my forehead, and the nightmares went away for good—until now, I mean. Would you do that for me?"

*Counselor:* "Well, I feel bad about your nightmares, but our church doesn't really do the kind of prayers you're talking about. Have you talked to your medical doctor about getting some tranquilizers?"

Correct ❑          Mistake ❑

Why? _____

_____

Write your own response: _____

_____

_____

_____

---

Actually, the use of religious symbols can be very helpful for a client in establishing a "point of contact" for his or her faith, to believe that what is hoped for can actually come true (Heb. 11:1). But the use of symbols, like the use of prayer, cannot be used to short-circuit the necessary work of the counseling process. It is not uncommon for Christian counselors to have clients referred to them by pastors from a number of churches who understand the use of their own symbols but do not understand the process of counseling. Their application of symbols will not work for their clients where there are complex underlying issues that have not been adequately explored. After adequate and appropriate counseling, the client is often ready to go back to his or her own pastor and have the same symbolic intervention successfully take place that previously failed due to premature use.

For a balanced presentation of the role of dramatic spiritual intervention in relation to counseling, see chapter 9.

## Mistake Number Nine: Poor Challenging Skills

*In one remarkable case that occurred at our clinic, the therapist was a psychologist intern from Rosemead Graduate School, Biola University. The client was a sales-and-marketing executive who had taken a number of courses on positive motivation, which he had found very helpful. However, he had gone on a spiritual detour, dabbling in the occult in an attempt to manipulate other people. He would regularly come to the counseling sessions with a sense of "magical thinking," in which he imagined his thoughts could control the thoughts of other people.*

*The task of the therapist was to detach this man's faith in the inappropriate occult practices and reattach his faith to the security of a Savior who had died for him and a Father, God, who loved and cared about him. The challenging skills employed in this case frequently took the form of directing the client to clearly determine cause-and-effect relationships in his attempts to motivate other people. During the course of the therapy, he was able to see that his most effective marketing and influencing came when he used his own natural charm and personality, undergirded by prayer. His significant failures occurred when he attempted to manipulate people at a distance through forms of mind control.*

As we approach the action-planning part of the counseling process, we are often called upon to challenge people to take bigger risks, set narrower boundaries, establish specific goals, or look more deeply into the motives behind their actions. Sometimes challenging takes the form of questions

such as why, when, and how. Other times, challenging is accomplished with leading statements or questions such as "Give me an example"; "How will that help?"; "What comes after that?"; or "Tell me what you expect as a result of that action." When we challenge people to examine their thought patterns, we need to be aware that we are going to make them uncomfortable.

Therefore, to avoid mistakes in challenging, it is important that challenging be precise, accurate, and timely. Yes-or-no questions, irrelevant comments, and inappropriate emphasis on secondary issues are common mistakes in the use of challenging skills. Also common among inexperienced counselors is the premature use of challenging, almost like debating, before adequate empathy and credibility is developed in the relationship between the counselor and the client.

For instance, as Christians, we know that miracles happen because of our faith (Matt. 9:29). It would be premature and inappropriate for us to challenge a client to "have faith" before knowing the deep issues of his or her life. We need to understand and be able to agree with the client about the area to which faith needs to be applied.

---

### 👋 Skill Builder 1.9

*Client:* "I know he's married, but he's the nicest boss I've ever had. I don't think he's *very* married . . . and when he just puts his hands on my shoulders, I feel like I want to be with him forever. . . . And now he's asked me to fly to Las Vegas with him next weekend!"

*Counselor:* "Tell me what you expect to happen in Las Vegas."

Correct ❑          Mistake ❑

Why? _____

_____

Write your own challenge statement: _____

_____

_____

_____

---

For an excellent pattern for positive challenging, see "Nick's Nine" in the section "Moving from Counselor to Coach" in chapter 6.

## Mistakes Number Ten and Eleven: Superficial Decisions and Artificial Action Plans

*During my second year of graduate school, I did an internship in counseling at Lakeview-Uptown Mental-Health Clinic in Chicago. One of my first clients was a twenty-eight-year-old gay man who specifically requested "a young, white, male therapist." As an inexperienced therapist with a ministerial back-ground, I tried in the first few interviews to evangelize Larry and lead him to Christ. He put equal energy into trying to get me to visit some gay bars with him so that I could "observe the lifestyle."*

*I had a history of leading people to the Lord. He had a history of seducing therapists (after first being seduced by his own psychiatrist at age fourteen). We listened courteously to each other, but when it came time for action plans, I could not get him to plan to go to church, and he could not get me to go to a gay bar. The "action plan" tests the sincerity and validity of the verbal thera-peutic exchange in a very practical way!*

*Once we realized that neither of us was going to accept the action plan of the other, we were forced to look at new issues and values on which we could agree to work together.*

You will find out what happened with Larry in chapter 6, "Advanced Action-Planning Skills."

At some point in every counseling experience, there comes a time to make decisions and create action plans. The point of decision occurs when the client decides what he or she wants to have happen in his or her life. The "action plan," based on that decision, lays out the map for how to make it happen. In a very real sense, the action plan is the part of the counseling enterprise that "tests the talk" that has occurred between the counselor and client up to this point. As Scripture teaches, "Faith by itself, if it does not have works, is dead" (James 2:17).

Two of the most common counseling mistakes regarding decisions and action plans made in counseling are:

a. keeping the counseling on a content or emotional level without ever coming to a decision or action plan; and
b. pushing the client to make a decision or create an action plan too soon in the counseling process, before emotions and values are sufficiently explored and clarified.

To avoid these mistakes, explore the client's emotions and values, not just content. Compare or contrast the client's values with Scripture. Then work as a coach, helping the client to create a realistic action plan based on values you can support and to which the client is committed.

**Skill Builder 1.10**

*Client:* "I just can't flunk out of this college and go home and tell my mom—she's worked night and day to pay my tuition, and I'm working seven nights a week to pay my room and board. Even though I don't like the other kids here very much, I don't want to go home and break her heart."

*Counselor:* "It sounds like you'll just have to drop out, at least for a while."

Correct ❏          Mistake ❏

Why? _____

_____

Write your own action plan: _____

_____

_____

_____

For more information on how to develop workable action plans, see chapter 6.

## Mistake Number Twelve: Overlooking Accountability

*Frank was a California surfer with a history of "flashing" police cars. He always got arrested. He had been in therapy several times but had always relapsed into this strangely self-destructive "addiction." He had never been in an aftercare or follow-up accountability program. His therapist introduced him to Sexaholics Anonymous, where he found a sponsor and a fellowship of people with whom he could be honest and who were willing to hold him accountable for his actions on a daily basis.*

Following a decision based on values, an action plan that implements that decision in a practical way is created. The final step is the selection and commitment to an accountability process. This step supports, reinforces, and maintains the new decision and the actions that go with it.

This step is frequently overlooked, and the person "relapses" and fails to follow through on an otherwise valid decision and workable action plan.

Methodist church founder John Wesley recognized this principle when he created his Saturday meeting group. Psychologist O. Hobart Mowrer utilized the same concept when he designed his Integrity Therapy program. Bill W., co-founder of Alcoholics Anonymous, incorporated this principle into steps 5–7 of the famous Twelve Steps. Accountability to you as the pastoral counselor is not enough! Each quality decision should be:

a. clearly endorsed by the client;

b. submitted *by the client* to God in prayer; and

c. communicated to at least one other significant individual.

A small accountability group, such as an AA meeting or church Bible study, can assist the client to hold to the decision and work through the action plan. Action plans often become emotionally or practically more difficult than anticipated.

Much of the strength of the early Christian church was due to the believers' strong sense of fellowship and accountability to each other. Following Peter's great evangelistic sermon, several thousand people committed themselves to meet regularly in small groups to share in prayer, Bible study, meals, and recreation (Acts 2:42). These actions reinforced their new Christian faith.

Our clients, who are often working through difficult emotional and spiritual issues, need and deserve the same quality and availability of support.

---

### 🖐 Skill Builder 1.11

*Client:* "Sometimes I think about committing suicide. I feel so depressed!"

*Counselor:* "Maybe you should read a positive Christian book."

Correct ❏        Mistake ❏

Why? _____

_____

Write your own response, including an accountability process: _____

_____

_____

See the section "Coaching for Independence" in chapter 6 for more information.

---

The final exercise for this chapter involves conducting and recording a practice counseling interview. Ask a friend, another student, or a family member to work with you on this exercise. Ask him or her to talk about something real (not role play!). The topic may be happy or sad, important or merely trivial, so long as it is real. The person who is serving as the client should talk, and you should practice responding, using some of the counseling techniques and principles highlighted in chapter 1.

To reduce any anxiety about being recorded, offer to return the tape cassette immediately following the interview if your practice client has said anything he or she does not wish to have on tape. The interview should be conducted for approximately five to fifteen minutes, with your tape recorder running. At the end of the interview, spend half an hour playing the tape back and making notes on the "Taped Interview Analysis" page about what you said and did. Include responses you feel were well stated as well as responses you feel could have been better. If you are using this manual in a classroom setting, make a list of questions that come to your mind as you review the recorded interview, and discuss these questions in class.

Chapter One **BACK TALK**

Please answer the following questions for this chapter:

1. What is the main point of this chapter? _____

_____

_____

2. What was your favorite story or illustration in this chapter? Why? _____

_____

_____

3. Describe a personal experience you have had as a counselor or counselee (formal or informal) that relates to the content of this chapter: _____

_____

_____

4. What questions do you have after reading this chapter? _____

_____

_____

5. What would you like to learn more about as you continue to read about counseling? _____

_____

## Chapter One **TAPED INTERVIEW ANALYSIS**

Name:_____

Date:_____

Interview Number:_____

1. What was the client's presenting (initial) problem or opportunity?_____

_____

_____

_____

2. What skills did you attempt to practice in this interview? Give one or more

examples: _____

_____

_____

_____

3. What do you feel you did best in this interview? _____

_____

_____

_____

4. What do you feel you need to improve upon based on this interview? ____

_____

_____

_____

5. Describe any surprises, shifts in direction or content, or significant positive

or negative turning points in this interview: _____

_____

_____

_____

6. How was the client thinking and/or feeling by the end of this interview? __

_____

_____

_____

7. If this were an interview series, what do you think might happen in the next interview?_____

_____

_____

_____

8. What did you learn most about the process of personal counseling from conducting this interview? _____

_____

_____

_____

## Chapter Two

**THE COUNSELOR'S LIBRARY**

Consider adding one or more of these books to your counseling library:

Collins, Gary R. *The Biblical Basis of Christian Counseling for People Helpers: Relating the Basic Teachings of Scripture to People's Problems.* Colorado Springs: NavPress, 1993.

> Dr. Collins is president of the International Institute of Christian Counseling. This user-friendly volume integrates sound theology and practical counseling principles.

Hunt, W. H. *How Can I Help?: A Christian's Guide to Personal Counseling.* Nashville: Thomas Nelson, 1994.

> A well-articulated six-lesson training program for Christian crisis counselors. This book is accompanied by six well-made videos that can be used in training your staff.

*Praise and Worship Study Bible,* New Living Translation. Wheaton, Ill.: Tyndale House, 1997.

> This fresh new translation is accompanied by special notes and prayers that will speak to the heart of your client and to your own heart as well.

Tournier, Paul. *Guilt and Grace.* New York: Harper and Row, 1958.

> This insightful book is the work of Swiss Christian physician Paul Tournier, who William Barclay says is "a man who is skilled in medicine and wise toward God." The book's concepts are especially helpful in sorting true moral guilt from neurotic, shame-based, false guilt.

Doc & Duck © 1999 Andrew J. Cheydleur

# Basic Interview Structure

EVERY INTERVIEW has a beginning, middle, and end. The purpose of this chapter is to introduce you to the basic steps of a brief, informal counseling session from the point of identifying the counseling opportunity through the close of the interview, including setting up further appointments as needed.

## Listening for the Opportunity

*Once I had an employment interview with a young woman who was looking for a position as a therapist in one of our group homes for retarded adults. She was a very bright person who was working for a small, underfunded Christian agency in northern California. She had written a book on weight loss and was intensely interested in the subject. Partway through our employment interview, I began to hear her great need to express her reactions to the lack of professional respect she was receiving in her current position.*

*I recognized the counseling opportunity in the midst of an otherwise normal employment interview. I responded by saying (another staff member was present), "I somehow feel like giving you a hug, but since that might not be appropriate, would you care to share with us a little of your hurt?" Although it "ruined" the employment interview, that caring invitation broke the spiritual and emotional logjam of her mind. The sorrows and cries of her heart gushed forth for the next forty-five minutes, allowing my associate and me to care about her as a person. We responded to her needs. Eventually, we shared some godly principles for enhancing her professional position in the agency where she was already employed, which she really did not want to leave.*

When should you do spiritual counseling? How will you find people who need your help? What about setting up appointments? These are typical questions that new pastoral-counselors-in-training ask. The answer is that there are people all around you who are asking for your help on a daily basis, if you will simply listen for the opportunity!

God loved the people of the world enough to send His Son, Jesus, to be our Savior, and He continues to care about people enough to commission us to be counselors and burden bearers for them.

When a man or woman comes to us and tentatively begins to open up buried feelings, frustrated emotions, or other needs, he or she is behaving toward us in a very meek fashion. Frank Damazio, in his comprehensive book *The Making of a Leader,* reminds us from Psalm 149:4 that God will beautify the meek with salvation. As counselors, we are God's agents to provide some of the positive results that God promises will come from the development of a meek spirit. Pastor Damazio has researched the fact that if we are sensitive and willing to hear the opportunity, God can use us to help those who make themselves meek before us in a number of ways:

- to eat and be satisfied (Ps. 22:26)
- to receive guidance in their judgments and decisions (Ps. 25:9)
- to be taught in the ways of God (Ps. 25:9)
- to inherit the earth (Ps. 37:11)
- to be saved (Ps. 76:9)

Although the client's surface attitude may not always appear to be meek, the very act of coming to us is a statement of meekness. This needs to be honored with attentive listening to the deep hurts and desperate search for goodness and God.

---

**Skill Builder 2.1**   In response to each of the following client statements or questions, jot down a phrase or sentence you might say to the client to identify this approach as a counseling opportunity.

A. "Excuse me, do you have a minute?" _____

_____

_____

B. "Everybody around here treats me like a machine." _____

_____

_____

C. "Do you think people can go to heaven if they commit suicide?" _____

_____

_____

D. "Sometime when it's convenient, I would like to discuss a problem that a friend of mine is experiencing." _____

_____

_____

E. "I want you to know that I would never say anything bad about my husband, but . . . " _____

_____

_____

## Asking Yourself, "Why Now?"

*An older woman was referred to our Christian clinic by the police. She had accused the local water company of trying to pump poison gas into her home to kill her! The "Why now?" search revealed that Anne was not really a classic paranoid. Her husband had been sick and bedridden for several years. He had died about six months prior to her referral to the clinic. Although it had been a tremendous burden to take care of him, she was now left with a deep void, great anguish, and loss. As a Christian, she could not admit to herself that she was thinking about suicide. Her desperation was reflected in the symbolism of the water company's trying to kill her.*

*Once our staff understood the answer to the "Why now?" question, they were able to proceed with the grief counseling that Anne's own church had failed to provide after the death of her husband. This eventually resulted in a very satisfactory and positive outcome with many productive years still available to quite a plucky and resourceful lady!*

Whether the person approaches us in an informal way or makes an advance appointment for a counseling interview, we need to remember and respect the process and/or crisis that has preceded his or her decision to request counseling at this particular point in time (the "Why now?" question). Sometimes this can be determined by listening to the client directly; sometimes the external circumstances reveal what has been going on; sometimes we are only able to identify the precursors of the counseling request by listening to the internal prompting of the Holy Spirit.

We know that God is on our side (Ps. 56:9), and as pastoral counselors, we are searching for the key that will allow us to be on the side of our client. God's Spirit can tell our spirit that we are His children (Rom. 8:16-17). His Spirit can also reveal to our spirit both the deep hurt and the potential fulfillment present within the spirit of the person we are counseling.

**Skill Builder 2.2**  For each of the following, jot down a "probe" or a "prompt" you could ask the client that would help you to answer the "Why now?" question.

A. "I have finally decided to get a divorce from my husband." _____

_____

_____

B. "Do you think I am too old to go back to college?" _____

_____

_____

C. "I think I'd like to have a baby." _____

_____

_____

D. "I think I've just been in this job too long." _____

_____

_____

E. "It's just too painful to stay in this relationship without being married."___

_____

_____

## Developing Spiritual Sensitivity

How do we train ourselves to be sensitive to the cry of the human spirit and the prompting of the Holy Spirit if we are to be effective and powerful spiritual counselors? Dennis and Matthew Linn and Sheila Fabricant, in their sensitive and useful workbook *Prayer Course for Healing Life's Hurts,* suggest that the key to our training may be found in Ezekiel 36:26: "I will give you a new heart and put a new spirit within you; I will take the heart of stone out of your flesh and give you a heart of flesh." They suggest a three-point exercise, which you may find helpful in unblocking the sensitivity of your own heart:

1. Let Jesus reveal to you one person you need to love and forgive.
2. Pick up an actual stone to represent the stony heart of the one you are trying to forgive.
3. Let your hands be the hands of Jesus, holding and loving the stony heart into a heart of flesh.

This can be a very vivid exercise. If you try it, keep your journal handy, jot down the insights you receive about yourself and the other person during this process, and then pray for that person.

The power of the "loving-a-stony-heart" exercise and the "Why now?" review in counseling both depend on your willingness to listen to God and the other person. Often you will find that you turn the corner of understanding in your counseling interview or interview series when you discover the answer to the "Why now?" question. You do this through your sensitive listening to the client and through the inner prompting of the Holy Spirit.

---

**Skill Builder 2.3**  For each of the following client statements, try to restate the material to the client in a sensitive way that captures both the emotion and the content he or she is trying to communicate.

A. *Client:* "I can't stand it anymore!"

You feel . . . _____

_____

B. *Client:* "My new job is going better than I have any right to expect."

You feel . . . _____

_____

because . . . _____

_____

C. *Client:* "I can't take on any more tasks right now; I am a little frazzled around the edges."

You feel . . . _____

_____

and . . . _____

_____

D. *Client:* "This whole office is ridiculous!"

You think . . . _____

_____

E. *Client:* "You are the only person who has shown me the least bit of caring in this whole rotten mess!"

You feel . . . _____

_____

## Changing Gears

*One of my counseling students told me about a woman who "bothered her" at church during most of the summer with various emotionally charged but objectively trivial concerns. The woman would approach just as my student was going to the platform to lead worship. Invariably my student spent a fair amount of time trying to disentangle herself from this person, arriving late to the platform for the worship service. She also set herself up to be "ambushed" the following Sunday in the same manner.*

Once you have recognized there is a counseling opportunity, you need to very rapidly "change gears" from whatever you were planning to do next into a counseling mode. Very often you will find that it takes less time to establish and complete a brief, five-minute counseling session than it does to attempt to disengage yourself from a wily, desperate, and emotionally clinging would-be client!

If my counseling student had quickly

determined this lady was a possible counseling opportunity, she could have turned directly to the woman, looked her squarely in the eye, and defined how much time she had available. She then could have given the woman her absolute, intense personal concentration for that period of time, sensitively reflecting everything the woman said without further comment or questions. She could also have established a future appointment during the week in a more structured and positive environment in which the lady's deeper concerns could have been explored. It is obvious that these concerns were "trial balloons" in an attempt to get the counselor's attention and interest.

You can practice changing gears in this fashion: Read a book or magazine, watch TV, or engage in any other kind of concentrated activity. First ask a friend or family member to come and "interrupt" you while you are doing this. Then see how quickly you can refocus your attention from the activity you were engaged in to the simulated interruption, converting it from being an interruption into an opportunity. (For a prime biblical illustration of this kind of changing gears, see Luke 10:25-37.)

---

**Skill Builder 2.4**   Practice changing gears by choosing one of the following activities:

- Read a magazine
- Watch television
- Read a book
- Other concentrated activity:_____

Ask a friend or family member to deliberately interrupt you while you are doing the above activity. Then give him or her your complete attention as quickly as possible. Write yourself a note about what the "client" said and how you responded.

The "client" said: _____

_____

I responded:_____

_____

---

## Introducing the Time Structure

*Suppose you were coming out of church and your friend Jim grasped your arm and said with great emotion, "Drat! The Giants lost again! That's just one more thing gone wrong in my life this week! Just seems like the last straw." You might immediately recognize this outburst as a counseling opportunity and begin to question what kind of process or crisis made the unfortunate Giants game become "the last straw" in this man's life. If you did, you could decide to change gears, then provide some significant care and attention to him.*

After changing gears, the first thing you need to do is to structure the interview time. You need to be honest with yourself about how much time you can really give. Suppose you have about a half-hour leeway before departing to be at someone's home for dinner. While you could go overtime and apologize to the host or hostess, the likelihood is that you couldn't give complete attention to the counseling in that event. So you could convey respect both to your own appointment schedule and to the hurting person by acknowledging this.

You might say, "Well, Jim, I have about a half hour that we could spend right now; would you like to go across the street to the coffee shop and talk to me about your week?" That would be positive, caring, and invitational. However, if you did it that way, you might find that Jim, now that he has your attention, doesn't want to break your attention even long enough to go across the street to the coffee shop. You could get trapped in the church lobby!

Whenever you are "interrupting" a client's self-talk with new information, you will have the best attention to your information if you place it within an "empathy sandwich." When you announce the time limit of the interview, you are introducing a new piece of information. An "empathy sandwich" is like a hamburger, except that instead of surrounding a meat patty with a bun, you are surrounding your new information with empathetic reflections of the client's self-statements. In this case the empathy sandwich could go something like this: "Jim, I can see that the Giants' loss has really gotten to you in a powerful way. I mean, you really seem quite shaken by it. I have about a half hour before I have to go to my lunch appointment, but if you would like, we could go to the coffee shop and talk about this. I really felt quite worried when you said that this was 'the last straw.' I just couldn't walk out of here without finding out what's going on."

The late Father Charles Curran, Ph.D., president of the American Catholic Psychological Association, taught me to use an empathy sandwich in relation to structuring time for brief interviews in informal settings. Somehow a potential client can hear and accept your need for structure and time limitation better if you are at the same time communicating that you hear and accept the intensity of his or her need for your immediate attention.

Unless we work in a highly structured clinic environment, much of the personal counseling that we will do must be initiated in ways that are somewhat sacrificial to us. As one of my counseling students put it, "There have been times when people approached me with something on their minds, but I didn't want to be interrupted, for I was on a schedule and never felt I really had the time." However, if we will learn not only to give our time but to

36

define the amount of time that we have to give, we may be able to initiate a number of "Isaiah-58" counseling relationships. The relationship begins with some small sacrifice on our part but ends with great benefit to the client.

The would-be spiritual counselor can be tempted on two sides. One is to want his or her own life to be so orderly that no "interruptions" are permitted. The other side of the temptation is to assume that we are required to give love so sacrificially that we can ask nothing of the client in return. We may even be afraid to ask the client to respect the needs of others for whom we may already be scheduled to care. The Bible teaches that we should be bold when we speak the Word of God (Acts 4:29-31). We need to be equally bold, though courteous and empathetic, in holding those who bring their desperate needs to us without benefit of a schedule to the realistic amount of time and caring that we have available. Having given the time and help which we are able to, we can, like the Good Samaritan, make an appointment to see the person at a later time and assure the client that his or her needs are continuing to be addressed.

 **Skill Builder 2.5** The purpose of this exercise is for you to practice building an empathy sandwich, which will include: (a) your reflection to the client of the client's content and emotion; (b) your statement to the client about the amount of time you have available and place in which you wish to see the client; and (c) your statement of emotional and spiritual concern for the client. Write each statement as if you were speaking to the client.

*Client:* "I am so upset about what is happening to my daughter, and I have just got to talk to someone about it today, because I am really terrified, and I don't know what to do!"

A. (The client's feelings)

You feel . . . _____

_____

_____

B. (Time available)

I have about . . . _____

_____

C. (Your concern for the client)

I feel . . . _____

_____

## Establishing a Give-and-Take Rhythm

*Once when I was auditing the case records at a Salvation Army Rehabilitation Center, I discovered that the center had recently hired a new second-shift counselor with a long history of solid personal recovery from alcoholism but who had limited academic counseling training. In reviewing his case notes, I noticed they fell into one pattern: "Well, _____, you know that recovery is a long difficult road, so I think it would probably help you if I shared a little bit of my own personal story."*

*While this counselor certainly did have an excellent personal story to share, his excitement about sharing it was so great that it made it almost impossible for him to listen to the clients' problems! In fact, I briefly considered the possibility of writing this counselor's own personal biography based on his case notes, due to the fact that there was much more information about him in the case notes than there was about his clients! Counseling is a process of give and take; before we can provide prescriptive solutions, or even useful examples, we need to know the client, not simply our own preconceived answers.*

Once the personal counseling process is initiated, we need to model a back-and-forth structure of client statement and counselor response. If the client does all the talking and you provide no response other than a few grunts and positive head shakes, he or she may have a welcome opportunity to vent a few emotions but will not be spiritually, socially, or psychologically healed. On the other hand, if you as the counselor do all the talking based on some preconceived idea of what is wrong with the client, you might have the right response for the wrong problem!

Counseling interns frequently ask, "How do you know when to give and when to take? What about sharing our own personal experiences?" At the beginning of a counseling relationship, a safe rule of thumb is that you do not share your own personal experiences. When you talk, you repeat the content and emotion you have just heard from your client, so he or she is assured you have correctly heard what has been said.

The classic example of premature guidance can be found in the book of Job. Job's counselors all counseled out of their personal needs and historical family backgrounds, perhaps because they did not actually know the source of Job's problems. Often, we do not know the source of a person's problems, particularly at the beginning of an interview or early in a series of interviews. Poor spiritual and moralistic counseling, in the absence of lively faith, extensive listening, and believing prayer on the part of the counselor, is worse than no counseling at all. It can push people into despair and suicide. It can shift their anger and grief away from their circumstances and onto God in such a way that meaningful emotional, spiritual, or physical recovery is rendered almost impossible.

In fact, the counseling process is not just about venting. It is not limited to mirroring emotion in a way that someone with Rogerian training might be taught to do. It is about looking for concrete word symbols that help the client to progress. The interview or series moves from discussing content to emotions to values and value conflicts and later to decisions that become the basis for action plans that build new and positive structures into the client's life.

Dr. Curran, in his insightful book *Counseling and Psychotherapy: The Pursuit of Values,* describes the relationship between the client as "speaker" and the counselor as "translator." This kind of groping for "specific symbols" adequate to a person's immediate, emotion-charged situation is one of the main aspects of the counselor's or therapist's skill. It is, in fact, a threefold process:

1. The client's own confused and "mixed up" effort to express him- or herself in the emotion-charged language of affect
2. The counselor/therapist's striving to understand this language and to respond in a more adequately symbolic or cognitive form
3. The client's hearing this, analyzing it in relation to his or her own affect-cognitive state, and deciding that it either does or does not fit

To understand Dr. Curran's point, imagine you are translating for a person with a very unusual language problem: he or she can speak only in English but can hear and understand only in French. Every time this person says something in English, you must repeat it in French before he or she can understand it! In counseling, when you paraphrase and repeat a person's spoken thoughts, you are helping that person to better understand him- or herself.

It is this sort of give-and-take process that must be developed if the counseling time is to have maximum value. In the absence of such a process, much time will be wasted wandering around, listening to emotions without attaching them to content, or giving advice that is not adequately related to the real problems the client may not yet have stated. Using the give-and-take model, you will find that your counseling is much more efficient in terms of time. Your clients will feel much more cared about, and the actual results will prove far more positive.

---

**Skill Builder 2.6** Practice your give-and-take skills by responding to the following client statement. Reflect the content ("You think . . .") and the emotion ("You feel . . .") of the statement, and define the value or value conflict ("You believe . . .") contained in the statement.

*Client:* "When I dropped out of the cadet school, I felt terrible because I thought God had deserted me, even though I was fantastically happy. I was marrying the girl of my dreams. All my friends told me I was doing the right thing."

A. (Reflect content)

You think . . . _____

_____

B. (Identify emotions)

You feel . . . _____

_____

C. (List values)

You believe . . . _____

_____

---

## Capping the "Ain't-It-Awful" List

> *"Pastor, I am having the most terrible day. Besides, my mother-in-law is coming to town tomorrow night. And my toe hurts. And I don't think anybody in this church has any love whatsoever. And I'm thinking about committing suicide as soon as I can figure out how. Are you listening to me?"*

One of the most frustrating experiences for the novice counselor is to have a client begin to make one of those extended "ain't-it-awful" lists.

The temptation for us, regarding people who frequently give us "ain't-it-awful" lists, is to mentally shut them off while attempting to look polite as they run their lists to the very end. This polite but nonincarnate response takes a great deal of our time and does absolutely nothing to help the client! While the man in the street might be honest enough about his lack of love to simply say "shut up," we do not have that option. We need to find an honest way to express the healing power of love that is so deep, so cutting and pointed, that the power of God breaks through. This wakes the person up to the fact that somebody *is* listening and that God *does* care!

When you hear someone begin one of those "ain't-it-awful" lists, don't say to yourself, "Ain't it awful? There he/she goes again!" Instead, interrupt the person with a sensitive summary statement that reflects and connects the content and emotion of the point he or she is trying to make, e.g., "You feel awful because nothing has gone right all day!" In order to do this effectively, begin to lovingly and silently pray for the intelligent use of the spiritual gifts, such as wisdom and knowledge. Pray that you may understand the significance of the list being rolled out. Pray for God to give you an intense love that can break through this desperate, ritualized recital of apparently disconnected items. Exercise the mental discipline to interrupt the list after every item, reflecting the essence of the item back to the speaker in an attempt on your part to understand the importance of that item.

As you intently listen to the Spirit of God speaking within your heart and use your own intelligent perception of what is going on, you will often be able to "cap" the list after only two or three items, penetrating to the symbolic "sum" of the speaker's list of items.

With this kind of intense listening and perception, you will save a great deal of time and frustration in counseling. Very often you will penetrate the ritualized facade that the client brings with his or her lists. This will enable you to move to the deep levels of hurt, frustration, and conflicted values that really underlie the process.

In the example above, the pastor could have saved a great deal of time by interrupting after the second or third item, saying, "You really seem to be having a bad day today." This summation would have taken away the client's necessity to continue to build a list until he or she realized that the counselor wasn't even listening. Very likely the conversation would have moved from list building to true counseling, with a deepening relationship between the client and the pastoral counselor.

The technique of summarizing and "capping" the list is simple, but the list must be capped with love rather than simply with mechanical feedback.

Of course, the lists we hear in counseling are not always "ain't-it-awful" lists. Some of them are "ain't-it-wonderful" lists, in which the client is trying to get a handle on a variety of experiences, hoping that the counselor will help him to translate them into some meaningful whole.

In these cases the counselees are asking you to "be Jesus" for them so that they can hear the kind of wisdom and affirmation that God would give if He were visibly present and physically accessible to them.

The person who comes to you with a long list of apparently unrelated items or a list of items that seem to be remote in time or circumstance can really be a bother. On the other hand, as believers, we choose to be kind to each other because God has forgiven us (Eph. 4:32). As counselors, we want to combine kindness and skill, spiritual sensitivity and effective intervention. Gently interrupting and skillfully capping your client's list is one of the kindest things you can do. It is one of the most effective ways you can move the counseling interview forward.

**Skill Builder 2.7** Jot down a statement or phrase you could use with each client that would summarize the list being presented.

A. *Client:* "I have been going to this church for six weeks, and not one person has said a pleasant word to me. Besides, the kind of music they sing here is really not my kind of music. Last week the preacher devoted his whole sermon to try and get me to give more money than I am already giving. It doesn't seem to me that the people here really have any enthusiasm in their worship. . . . "

_____

_____

_____

B. *Client:* "It was a glorious weekend! Even though I only met him last week, I never had more fun with anybody in my whole life! Dancing was wonderful, sharing cotton candy was a new experience, the stars were brighter than I have ever seen them before. I felt like we could have been together forever. . . . "

_____

_____

_____

## Avoiding the Question Trap

*While I was attending graduate school, my friend Brian was working as a gang-outreach worker for The Salvation Army in Chicago. He enlisted my help to do some family counseling with the parents of some of the young gang members he was working with. One couple was particularly interesting. They were from a stable, Roman Catholic, blue-collar family. Al worked in an industrial job all day, stopped briefly at the tavern on the way home, and mostly watched TV before he went to bed. Maggie really ran the family. Their teenaged son had dropped out of school to escape his mother's influence and was living alone in the basement of an apartment building. He was also running with a gang and ignoring most of his family's values.*

*In the first interview, Maggie had a number of questions: What were my qualifications? Why couldn't the police do anything? Did I approve of the way her boy was living? and many others. My temptation was to try to field these various questions and give her satisfactory answers. The classes I was taking were teaching me to reflect the genuineness and emotional intensity of these concerns without getting caught up in prematurely answering questions. Al, who was present at the first interview, was passive during most of the first thirty to forty minutes while his wife tried to get me to answer questions. I tried to be empathetic without being caught up in providing answers that I wasn't qualified to give.*

*Maggie asked me, "Do you think my boy has a deep-seated psychological problem?" and I ducked by responding, "So you feel it would be helpful for you to know what I think about his mental status?"*

*Finally, tired of watching his wife's manipulations, Al pounded his fist on the desk and said to me, "I don't know what all this d___ counseling is supposed to do! Somebody needs to go and tell that kid he has to come home and go to school tomorrow morning!" And he did just that! After the interview, Al went to his son's apartment house and told him the facts of life. The son returned home and resumed school.*

*If I had tried to answer Maggie's questions, I would have participated in her "game" without being able to provide answers that would have adequately addressed the situation. Instead, because I did show my genuine caring, love, and respect for the tragedy of the situation, Al heard the need for somebody to address that tragedy not only with love but with the legitimate authority of a parent. Although he remained quiet during our counseling session, he participated by listening, and he eventually decided that he should give as much love, respect, and commitment to what was happening with his son as I was giving. He heard the content and emotions, processed the values, made a decision, and acted on it!*

Sometimes there are legitimate questions a client will ask you in counseling. If the same question comes up in more than one session, you may want to briefly answer it or refer the person to an appropriate information source. However, you want to avoid answering early information questions when you do not yet understand the emotional loading and spiritual significance they may have.

What's this all about?

Also, try to avoid *asking* too many informational questions that may create premature focus upon a particular point about which you are seeking information. Instead, allow the interview to flow in a progressive fashion toward the area of greatest concern.

The intelligent use of the spiritual gift of discernment will help you sort out the legitimate questions from those that are illegitimate or of lesser importance.

It is not unusual for a client to ask a question about your opinion on a moral or social issue. Often these questions are designed to rule you in or out as an acceptable, trustworthy, compassionate source of counseling. To directly answer questions like these during the early stage in the interview is to risk sabotaging the entire counseling process. While your opinion is important, ultimately the only thing that will be important is the way in which God's Spirit speaks to the person you are counseling. At later stages in an initial interview, or at later interviews within a longer-term counseling relationship, you will find it easier to determine the emotional and spiritual significance of the questions being asked. Then you may feel more free to respond directly to the questions. It is important, however, after answering a question, to give the client a chance to respond to the answer with either acceptance or rejection. Then you and the client can be very clear about his or her feelings and reactions to the information being presented.

---

**Skill Builder 2.8** Respond to each of the following questions by reflecting the question and giving dignity to the sincerity of the client—without answering the question.

A. *Client:* "How do you feel about people who drink?" _____

_____

_____

B. *Client:* "If I have AIDS, can I go to heaven?"

_____

_____

_____

C. *Client:* "Have you ever met someone who was a lesbian but decided to become a heterosexual?" _____

_____

_____

_____

D. *Client:* "How do you feel about abortion?"_____

_____

_____

_____

## Moving the Interview Deeper

*A friend of mine, a very gifted Christian therapist, had a client with an unusual dream. This man dreamed there was a giant fish traveling under the sidewalk on the street where he lived. The fish turned underneath the walkway leading up to the man's house, buckling the concrete plates and tunneling into the basement. The fish came up through the house, buckling the walls of the house and eventually punching a large hole through the roof! Definitely a disruptive dream!*

*While not every counselor is an interpreter of dreams, the process my friend used is very common in keeping any interview or counseling relationship moving forward.*

*In discussing his client's dream about the disruptive fish, my friend listened to the content while empathizing with the man's distress about what the dream symbolized. Later, he helped him reconstruct the dream as a parable of his own life, in which a recent decision to follow Christ had actually proved to be disruptive to all of his normal middle-class routines.*

*This man had a family who was not sure if he had become a fanatic. He had economic activities that were causing him financial loss because he had changed his business practices for moral reasons. He also was experiencing other kinds of conflicting situations between his previous personal life and his new life in Christ. Indeed, the fish symbolized Christ, not in His healing and loving aspect, but in His disrupting aspect of that which is too comfortable in our life. Having been put in touch with the value conflicts within his own current life, the client then needed to make some more conscious decisions between various values that were tugging him in more than one direction.*

A Christian therapist who believes that Christ has the power to save everyone that believes (John 1:12-13) and who believes that Jesus is the Bread of Life

(John 6:35) who sustains all believers, also believes that Jesus is sufficient to help every client work through the counseling process with a positive outcome. However, there is a definite process by which a person moves from the initial pain and confusion to a positive outcome that results in actions that redeem and benefit the individual, enhance relationships, and glorify God.

While at first *empathy* is most important, the accurate reflection of *ideas* is also important since *content* and *emotion* are used to understand the competing values in a client's life. We then look at values in conflict and eventually discuss decisions between values based on a biblical faith. Values that may be in conflict can include personal values, cultural values, and biblical values.

Once one has reached this level of a counseling relationship, it is important that the various conflicts between personal values and the values of others, as well as cultural values and biblical values, be adequately identified prior to any substantive decision making and action planning. During this process, the faith-based counselor will employ the sensitive use of Scripture to help a person define and resolve a value conflict.

See Continuing Education 102, "Scripture-Based Values," for additional help in this area.

 **Skill Builder 2.9**  In order to experience what this kind of deep listening might be like for another person, you may wish to try one of the many beautiful exercises recommended by the Linn Brothers in their marvelous workbook.

1. Using a separate sheet of paper, write down what is in your heart. Write as if you were writing a love letter to your best friend—Jesus—sharing what you feel most deeply. Don't worry about having the "right" words; only try to share your heart.
2. Now get in touch with Jesus' response to you, as He is already speaking to you. You might do this by asking what are the most loving words that you want Him to say to you. Imagine that what you have just written is a note to you from the person you love most and that you want to respond in the most loving possible words.
3. Write Jesus' response. Perhaps it will be just one word or one sentence. You can be sure that anything you write, if it helps you to know you are loved, is not just your own thoughts or imagination but is really what Jesus wants to say to you. (If you are finding this exercise difficult, you may want to copy passages from the Psalms or from one of the Epistles of John, which express Jesus' love to you. Add in some reflection of the content and emotion you wrote in one of these exercises.)
4. One or two people in the group (if you are doing this exercise in a group) might want to share what they have written with the whole group. During the companion sharing time that follows, companions may wish to share what they have written with each other.

## Keeping It All Together

*When I was a junior at Abington High School in Pennsylvania, I went to my guidance counselor for some input about college admissions. Mrs. Mackey explained the three-college "bracket" theory for getting admitted and told me which college would be best for me.*

*She was very knowledgeable, but I didn't use any of her information. Instead, I had a difficult freshman year at Swarthmore College. She failed to ask me how my parents and I felt about her recommendations, so she was not able to help us work through our resistance to the knowledge that would have helped us make a better choice.*

A new temptation surfaces when information begins to be important in the counseling process and the client and counselor are almost ready to undertake action planning. The temptation is for the counselor to want to move from counseling to teaching. Teaching is a very gratifying activity, but teaching is not counseling. The glue that continues to hold the counseling process together, even when much information is present and must be discussed, is cognitive and emotional empathy and "translation work." The counselor explores the client's feelings in order to integrate the new information.

The temptation to move from counseling to teaching is not uncommon. Even within counseling there are certain aspects of teaching and the introduction of new information, such as specialized Scriptures, that should be done. However, every bit of information needs to be introduced within an empathy sandwich, similarly to the way the original time structure was introduced. Also, the counselor will distance him- or herself from the information sufficiently to allow and respect a negative reaction by the client to any new informa-

Your ... blah blah repressive blah blah ... attitude blah blah blah manifests blah blah symptomatology blah blah blah somatic blah blah ...

tion. If the counselor grows overstimulated by one thought or overidentifies with the information he or she is presenting, he or she may either lose the ability to concentrate on what comes next or lose the attention and trust of the client.

Sometimes an interview will run down, and the counselor will not feel like expending any more energy or concentration on the client. If this becomes the case, it should be frankly stated, and a new appointment should be scheduled.

Additionally, while one of the aspects of good counseling is to be sensitive to your own emotional reactions, you also need to refrain from immediately transmitting them. Instead, hold them aside to be transmitted at a later point in the interview when you have developed a careful and prepared purpose for helping the interview move forward.

The counselor, in continuing to make a commitment to hear and care about what the client says, models the scriptural idea of giving thanks in everything (1 Thess. 5:18). In teaching we do not lose the intense need that the other person has for us to be comforting along with the teaching (1 Thess. 5:9-11). Also, in hearing a variety of ideas, the counselor does not get triggered by emotional words or threatening concepts and thereby seduced into arguments that result in "putting down" the client. As spiritual counselors, we do not speak evil about the client in the counseling session, nor do we discuss anything negative about him or her outside the area of counseling (1 Pet. 3:9-10).

Consider the following scenario:

> Client: *"I want a divorce from my husband, Tim."*
> Counselor: *"So you want to get divorced. How long have you been married?"*
> Client: *"I've been married twenty-three years, but I'm tired of him now."*
> Counselor: *"So you're tired of your marriage. What does God's Word say about this?"*
>
> *(One hour later)*
> Client to husband: *"Tim, I talked to my counselor, and she said I should get a divorce from you."*

The purpose of counseling is not for us to be understood but for us to be able to understand the client's needs, the Spirit of God, and the principles of Scripture in such a way that the client can incorporate them all together in one package.

If, at some point partway through this process, we are not being understood or are even being misrepresented outside the counseling sessions by the client, we do not need to feel alarmed, because our desire for the good of the client means we are suffering for Christ (1 Pet. 4:16).

We know that every step in the healing process can open up fresh pain. We do not take any step for granted, and we continue to care intensely about every word, emotion, and decision that our client is making. We are willing to communicate that intensity to the client with regular, frequent feedback.

See chapter 3 for listening principles and specific Skill Builders.

## Planning for Action

*In counseling an obese graduate student who was interested in losing weight, all the information appeared right, the emotions seemed to have been explored, and the values seemed to have been worked through and were in agreement with Scripture; however, we could find no agreement on the actions to be taken.*

*The first negotiated action commitment that was actually followed through by the client seeking weight loss was a decision/action to take a vitamin pill each morning! Obviously, taking a vitamin pill will not itself cause weight loss, but sometimes there must be a negotiated decision/action that can be carried out on a smaller level before the client can gain enough hope, faith, and belief to attempt actions that will impact on a larger level.*

Once the interview or interview series has moved to the point of genuine, deep, Scripture-based value decisions that the person is willing to own individually, there is still a further step.

These value decisions must be converted into action plans and worked out as activities in normal life outside the counseling relationship. Ultimately, it is the actions that confirm a personally satisfying solution based on biblical perspectives and value choices. As value decisions are converted into actions, a trialogue takes place between the client, the counselor, and God. Various action options are explored, weighed, rejected or accepted, experimented with, and tried again.

It is very easy for the counselor to get trapped into prescribing actions while the counselee becomes a passive consumer, "daring" the counselor to magically cure him or her. This will never work! The counselee must maintain a commitment to the process. This is easy at the beginning when he or she is being massaged by the counselor's acceptance of the client's emotions, but it remains important as the end approaches, when he or she must make actual proposals and choices of actions and then must commit to doing them.

Some clients (and some counselors!) will want to believe a

type of Gnostic heresy in which they think that having the right thoughts ends the process of counseling and that actions are not important. However, actions have great value, not only in confirming decisions but in creating positive responses from other people, which helps to reinforce a client in a new positive pattern of belief, reason, and behavior.

See chapter 6 for a number of concrete action-planning techniques and Skill Builders.

## "But I Have Just One Last Thing"

*Jesus made Lazarus rise from the dead by telling him to come out, even though everyone around knew that Lazarus had been three days in the grave and didn't seem to have much prospect of life. You will be surprised to see your counseling interview resurrected when you announce the time remaining!*

As an experiment, try this in your taped interview: If you originally told the person you only had ten minutes available, announce that there are only two minutes left when you are eight minutes into the interview! You may feel uncomfortable and mechanical the first time you try this, but you will be affirmed when, following this announcement, there will almost always be "one last thing"! If you fail to announce the time remaining in the interview

in advance, you will almost always have the client announce that he or she has "one last thing" when the interview actually should be over.

Many times you will find that people save the most critical thing in the interview for the "one-last-thing" time period.

By announcing the time remaining, you respect both the client and the integrity of the interview process. Of course, while you are counseling the client, it means you have to discipline yourself to wear a watch or be somewhere where you can see a clock. Practice this with someone in a nonthreatening situation, and you will be amazed at how your counseling interview becomes resurrected!

# Next!

> *"Well, I guess it really has been a surprise for you to find out that Sam was just not your friend but was also a boy! It does sort of affect your trust level in the relationship, and I think we are probably going to want to talk about that a bit more. Would next Wednesday after school at three-thirty be convenient?"*

Close your taped practice interview by setting up the next appointment. This method of closing the interview by opening the next appointment keeps the person from feeling rejected. It keeps the counselor from being manipulated by the client and takes "the moral higher ground" so the client does not have an excuse for prolonging the current interview.

## Trust the Process

If you follow the above process, both with your individual spontaneous interviews and more structured interview series, you will receive respect as a counselor. You will be better able to relax and to allow the Spirit of God to flow within the interview. In addition, you will be less likely to "throw away" brief counseling opportunities. You will experience an increased personal and spiritual satisfaction as the outcomes for your clients become more socially and spiritually successful.

Practice these principles as you work through the Skill-Builder exercises. Then experience their validity as you utilize them within your own tape-recorded practice interview sessions with a friend or family member.

Remember to instruct your practice client that he or she should talk about something real (not role play). Practice the time and structure techniques you have been learning, even if they seem awkward at first. After you complete your interview, review it using the "Taped Interview Analysis" page.

Chapter Two **BACK TALK**

Please answer the following questions for this chapter:

1. What is the main point of this chapter? _____

_____

_____

_____

2. What was your favorite story or illustration in this chapter? Why? _____

_____

_____

_____

_____

3. Describe a personal experience you have had as a counselor or counselee (formal or informal) that relates to the content of this chapter: _____

_____

_____

_____

_____

4. What questions do you have after reading this chapter? _____

_____

_____

_____

_____

5. What would you like to learn more about in the rest of this book? _____

_____

_____

_____

_____

Chapter Two **TAPED INTERVIEW ANALYSIS**

Name: _____

Date: _____

Interview Number: _____

1. What was the client's presenting (initial) problem or opportunity?_____

_____

_____

_____

2. What skills did you attempt to practice in this interview? Give one or more

examples: _____

_____

_____

_____

3. What do you feel you did best in this interview? _____

_____

_____

_____

4. What do you feel you need to improve upon based on this interview? ____

_____

_____

_____

5. Describe any surprises, shifts in direction or content, or significant positive

or negative turning points in this interview: _____

_____

_____

_____

6. How was the client thinking and/or feeling by the end of this interview? __

_____

_____

_____

7. If this were an interview series, what do you think might happen in the next interview?_____

_____

_____

8. What did you learn most about the process of personal counseling from conducting this interview? _____

_____

_____

Chapter Two **THE COUNSELOR'S LIBRARY**

Consider adding one or more of these books to your counseling library:

Curran, Charles. *Counseling and Psychotherapy: The Pursuit of Values.*
Apple River, Wis.: Apple River Press, 1975.
> You may need to visit a major university library to find this book, which is no longer in print, but it will be worth the search. One of the best pastoral-counseling books ever written.

Damazio, Frank. *The Making of a Leader.* Portland, Ore.: Bible Temple
Publishing, 1988.
> As C. Peter Wagner states in his forward, this book is "cutting edge" in its focused, Scripture-based approach to the training of pastoral leadership in the church.

Linn, Dennis, Matthew Linn, and Sheila Fabricant. *Prayer Course for Healing Life's Hurts.* New York: Paulist Press, 1983.
> This sensitive workbook offers more than one hundred practice exercises for fine-tuning your understanding of self, God, and your ministry to others.

The New King James Version of the Bible. Nashville: Thomas Nelson, 1979.
> This excellent new translation of the Bible retains the King James literary format while utilizing the newest scholarship.

Doc & Duck © 1999 Andrew J. Cheydleur

# Basic Listening Skills

*What would you do if you were confronted, as I was, by Mike, a huge, angry mechanic who came uninvited to my home one night with a bicycle chain that he wanted to wrap around my neck? In times like these we can call the police, recite thirty-four Scripture verses, or attempt to determine which counseling skills might be appropriate. Or we can place our spirit in tune with God and attempt to understand the bitter distress of the individual we are confronted with, just as Elisha listened to the bitter distress of the woman whose son had died (2 Kings 4:27).*

*At the beginning, my personal survival depended upon my ability to listen and to accurately reflect the emotions and personal concerns of this "client."*

*However, Mike's anger could not have been healed simply by the use of empathy skills or by my skillfully tying affect and cognition together. This healing also could not have taken place through the use of any of the other skills or experiences I had spent so much time and energy acquiring. The healing came as I was able to surrender my fear to God and allow His love to flow through me and melt the tremendous anger that covered a broken heart and deeply troubled life.*

THE PROCESS of faith-based spiritual counseling requires us to listen to God as we listen to the client, allowing God to guide us in the use of our natural abilities, learned skills, and spiritual gifts in order that we can restore hope, faith, and love to the brokenhearted (2 Cor. 1:3-4).

In concrete terms, you practice this process by first listening and then reflecting the client's content and, if possible, reflecting his or her emotion.

If you can, you then reflect content married to emotion, i.e., "You feel _____, because _____."

As the interview progresses, you listen even more deeply to the client (while you depend on the Holy Spirit), seeking to determine what the client believes (or values deeply) about the situation under discussion. Then you verbally reflect: "It appears that you believe she was unfair in the situation, when you expected her to be merciful."

In our interviews we try to listen for and reflect all three levels: content, emotion, and value. Not all of these levels are present in every statement or even in every interview.

However, during counseling-skills training, it is not uncommon for students to focus so strongly on skill development that, for a time, they seem to lose a clear sense of the deeper purpose of the counseling process. As one counseling student stated, "All I can think about is whether or not I'm saying the right things." Without a continuous awareness of the love of God flowing through us, the most carefully developed counseling skills will appear as mere mechanical manipulations, or as Scripture states, "sounding brass" or a "clanging cymbal."

*Medical psychiatry* seeks to repair the mind-body connection by selecting the correct medication to repair the way a person's brain functions. *Clinical psychology* seeks to identify and reconcile the discrepancies between an individual's emotional reaction(s) and the reality of the situation(s) the person needs to make choices about and deal with. A third professional counseling discipline, *clinical social work,* seeks a reconciliation between the person and the social environment.

Professional pastoral counseling often includes the concerns of other counseling disciplines, but the purpose is holy and requires a more complex sensitivity than the other three approaches. The focus of spiritual counseling is nothing less than the reconciliation of the three dimensions of life (mind, body/emotions, and social environment) with the powerful and critical fourth dimension of the spirit.

In a broad sense, *insanity* might be defined as the lack of "match" or "fit" between any of the four dimensions of life listed above. The various forms of counseling are attempting to restore sanity by bringing one or more of these back into congruence with the others.

However, when we serve as counselors, we are commissioned by God to serve as His representatives to heal the hurting. God promises that He is "near to those who have a broken heart" (Ps. 34:18) and that He "heals the brokenhearted and binds up their wounds" (Ps. 147:3). The deep, caring, searching heart of God understands that the lack of congruence in our life is not simply a mechanical thing to be fixed, as though we were an assemblage of auto parts! God feels the deep distress of the individual and understands that shame and reproach can break a heart (Ps. 69:20). God knows that the emotions of heartbreak also affect the spirit (Prov. 15:13) and can destroy physical health as well (Prov. 17:22).

It is important that our deep desire and purpose in pastoral counseling be to heal the brokenhearted rather than to acquire a series of techniques or some type of system to use in order to make it easier to keep people at a distance.

Leanne Payne, one of today's most gifted Christian therapists, states:

> The concept of listening to God and moving in the power and author-ity He gives to heal is strangely alien to many modern Christians. They have become dependent upon medical science for their healing needs, and upon the secular (both rational and occult) psychologies and therapies devised for gaining personal wholeness. Wherever true schol-arship informs the study of man, the resulting insight and procedural skills are to be received by the Christian with thankfulness. To his own peril will he ignore such wisdom and experience. Much of the wisdom, in fact, the Church has had at one time, but has since forgotten or ignored it."

The better we become at spiritual counseling, the less pride we will take in it. Every time God uses us to release joy in a previously troubled person, we will realize that the power that has healed the person is of God and does not stem from our righteousness or ability. It is most effective when we empty ourselves and allow God to bring healing and wholeness through us.

Somehow, in times of emergency, we intuitively understand that we are not the source of the cure but that we must depend on God Himself. However, it is in the apparently less intense experiences that we must also find a way to hear the Spirit of God. This allows God to structure and define the counseling experience so that it can be most effective in meeting the needs of clients.

 **Skill Builder 3.1** In this Skill Builder, you will practice three skills-training techniques: the "parrot," the "computer," and the "emotional mirror." Complete the Skill Builder, then try these with a friend or family member.

### EXAMPLE

*Client:* "I've had such a frustrating day. They canceled my health insurance and didn't even write me in advance. Now I need to go to the hospital."

*Counselor*—Parrot (almost exact words, but in second-person voice): "You've had a frustrating day. They canceled your health insurance and didn't write you in advance. Now you have to go to the hospital."

*Counselor—Computer* (content without emotion): "Your health insurance has been canceled, and now you need to go to the hospital."

*Counselor—Emotional Mirror* (emotion without content): "You're frustrated, angry, and scared."

PRACTICE

*Client:* "My project at work is behind schedule. I'm trying to put on a brave front, but I'm afraid. I might not be able to get it done. I just don't need another failure in my life."

*Counselor—Parrot* (almost exact words, but in second-person voice): _____

_____

_____

_____

*Counselor—Computer* (content without emotion): _____

_____

_____

_____

*Counselor—Emotional Mirror* (emotion without content):_____

_____

_____

_____

## Listening to the Three Spirits

*One of my earliest experiences in "hearing the three spirits" (the spirit and emotions of the client, the spirit and emotions of the counselor, and the guidance and caring of the Holy Spirit) came when I was nineteen and working as a counselor at a Christian summer camp. A teenaged girl on the maintenance staff sought me out during a weekend break when there were no children in camp and told me that her boyfriend had stalked off into the woods, saying that he was going to commit suicide! Having at this point taken two college courses in psychology (one in perceptual psychology and one in learning theory) and knowing very little Scripture, I was hardly prepared to be the counselor that she needed! However, I tried to sympathetically listen as she told me the story of how her boyfriend had come to visit her and told her that everything was going wrong with his life and that he simply wanted to die.*

*As I listened, I certainly did get in touch with her desperate love and genuine concern for his safety. I also listened to my own sense of insecurity, fear of doing or saying the wrong thing, and desire to help in any way that I could (if only I could think of a way!). However, there were three voices, not two, speaking that day, and I distinctly felt the Holy Spirit telling me that if I would be courageous enough to pray with her, her boyfriend would turn back from his quest to commit suicide in the woods. I verbally prayed that God would take away every emotion and thought that plagued her boyfriend and make him only think of her, of life, and of returning safely to her. The Holy Spirit supplied the ingredient that would have been missing had this only been a dialogue! He supplied the specific type of prayer to be prayed and the way to pray. We later learned that at the very moment we prayed, her boyfriend felt an overwhelming urge to stop, turn around, and stand still, facing back down the trail toward the camp. He returned to her, asking her forgiveness for thinking only of his own sorrow and not of their life that they were planning together.*

Much later, I took a seminar at Northwestern University, where I learned a more systematic approach to suicide intervention, based on the research of Schneidman and Farberow in their excellent book *The Cry for Help.* Yet in my early ignorance, the Holy Spirit still showed the right thing to do to meet that desperate need.

When we listen attentively to the client's spirit, we listen for emotions and feelings, for reasons and facts, and we especially listen for faith and beliefs (as well as misbeliefs).

As we try to become aware of our own spirit, we pay special attention to our own body language, which shows us whether we are closing or opening up to the client. We listen to our emotional reactions to the client as a person, as well as to our own faith and beliefs.

The mind of the Holy Spirit speaks to our mind during the counseling experience. We seek to be particularly open to the spiritual awareness of unknown facts (the gift of knowledge) and scriptural principles that apply (the gift of wisdom). We attempt to be open to those prayer promptings and nudges that come to us from the Spirit, and we listen for specific Scriptures or other special words or interventions that God will lead us to use with the client.

> *One of my pastoral counseling students, who had worked for some time in a residential rehabilitation center, stated, "I've spent a lot of time listening to men talk about their feelings and situations and how they got where they are. In the midst of listening to them, I always seemed to hear the Holy Spirit giving me the right things to say."*

Of course, learning to hear the differences between our spirit and the Holy Spirit is essential to the integrity and usefulness of the process.

**Skill Builder 3.2**   Imagine you are counseling a middle-aged pastor who says he wants to be divorced from his wife, to whom he has been married for twenty-five years. As you read the following paragraph, first think about what he is saying; then imagine what your internal "voice" might say to you if you were counseling such a person. Then imagine what the voice of the Holy Spirit might say to you on such an occasion.

*Client:* "I am so frustrated; I think I have to get out of this marriage. My friends who are pastors tell me that she has been a drag on my career for many years, and I am never really going to go anywhere as long as I am married to her. She gets kind of crazy at times, and she doesn't want to do any of the normal things that a pastor's wife is expected to do. The more I think about it, the more it seems to me that it was probably not God's will for me to marry her in the first place, so that by getting divorced, I would actually be returning to God's will. Then, perhaps God could bring the right woman into my life."

A. What are some of the key things that this man is saying? _____

_____

_____

B. What are your internal reactions as a person and as a counselor? What thoughts come to you as you read the above paragraph? _____

_____

_____

C. Imagine what the Holy Spirit might say to you if you were counseling this man. _____

_____

_____

## First Level: Listening

*A young professional woman came to see me for counseling. Sue made it clear during the first interview that she "didn't want to be a Christian." Much of the material she presented during the first interview had to do with her relationships and social environment. Her brother was a drug addict, and most of the young men she knew wanted to do cocaine whenever she went to their parties. Her disjointed emotions were a result of her mind telling her that the people she socialized with and their behaviors were not stable or helpful to her.*

*As is common, the lack of match between what her mind told her and what her social environment was presenting was displayed as pain, confusion, and uncertainty. For other people, lack of congruence might also be reflected as a lack of respect for self or others or in various forms of dishonesty with self or others. It seemed the only "straight" people this young lady knew were "born-again Christians," but she did not want to be thought of as a religious fanatic or identify with them. The problem for Sue was that everyone else she talked to seemed to have some sort of "angle" or selfish interest. She had even called the county crisis line to complain about the way she was being manipulated by men, and the "counselor" asked her if she wanted to come and sleep over in his apartment to get away from the more manipulative people she was describing!*

*Sue, who was coming to see me on a monthly basis, continued to struggle with her desire to be with "good" people while most of the time putting herself in environments where there were very few prospects for that to occur. After about six months of these approximately-once-a-month appointments, often scheduled in a somewhat impetuous fashion, she stated, "My friends said I shouldn't come to you, since you were a Christian counselor and all you would do is quote the Bible and tell me I was a bad person. Frankly, I am a little surprised that you haven't once quoted the Bible, or asked me to pray to be forgiven of my sins, or anything like that!"*

*Of course, the reason that I had not done anything spiritually overt was that I had been listening to her fearful spirit and to the Holy Spirit's cautioning voice. During the next session, I was able to lead this beautiful young lady to the Lord, and she was soon able to find a spiritually supportive church where she could meet the kind of positive young people she had been talking about for the last six months!*

It is easy for an "interview" to function like a conversation—polite and pleasant and providing no healing or reorganization—or to stay focused on content, with one question after another, like a TV interview. To go deeper than this level, we seek to listen for congruence (a good fit) or lack of congruence (a bad match) between the person's feelings and emotions and the three other dimensions:

1. Mind/reasons/facts
2. Spirit/Scripture
3. Social environment/relationships

Depending on which dimensions of a person's life clash with each other, a person might also express a continuous expectation of poverty or a denial of very real poverty; or he or she may express doubt about God or the value of life. Other elements that may be clues to a lack of congruence are biblical illiteracy, recurrent preventable physical sickness, lack of prayer, a sense of grief and loss without a specific focus, undifferentiated anger, etc.

Dramatic successes are sometimes possible with effective counseling that takes into account your spirit, the client's spirit, and the wise counsel of the Holy Spirit.

They show why the combination of spiritual intuition and skill acquisition is critical, because even when you do everything right, you will still not have success in every case. Therefore, be gentle with yourself as you develop your counseling skills, and do not expect every person to get well instantly.

See chapter 4 for additional information on connecting content and emotion together in your listening and reflection time with clients.

---

**Skill Builder 3.3**  Based on the information in Skill Builder 3.2 as well as your own reactions and what you have imagined the Holy Spirit might say to you in this circumstance, answer the following questions.

A. In what ways do the person's feelings "match" or "fit" with the facts he/she presents? _____

_____

_____

_____

B. Where is there a lack of "fit" or "match" between the person's emotions and the dimension of mind/reasons/facts?_____

_____

_____

_____

C. Is there a good "fit" between the person's feelings and emotions and the dimension of Spirit/Scripture? How or how not? _____

_____

_____

_____

D. How do the person's feelings and emotions fit with the dimension of social environment/relationships? _____

_____

_____

_____

E. Is there any lack of "match" between the person's feelings and emotions and the dimension of Spirit/Scripture? How or how not? _____

_____

_____

_____

F. Is there any lack of "match" between the person's feelings and emotions and the dimension of social environment/relationships? If so, what? _____

_____

_____

_____

G. What kinds of expectations and beliefs does the client seem to have in this illustration?_____

_____

_____

_____

## Second Level: Probing

*A young science teacher, a relatively new Christian, left his teaching position. He was very depressed and felt he was a bad person because of recurrent masturbation. Had I, as the counselor, immediately focused on this behavior in a negative or positive way, we would never have arrived at the real source of his depression. The young man's bringing up the subject of masturbation was actually a clue to the real issue, which was of a sexual nature. In order to test the counselor's perception, acceptance, and skill, a person in counseling will often discuss something less important that is "in the area" of his or her primary concern.*

*After a number of interviews in which the counselee seemed to want to detour into endless arguments about whether God was good or simply liked to manipulate people, he revealed that the reason he had left his position as a teacher was that he had a drunk driving conviction! When gently probed to further discuss this, he revealed that he had been "thrown in jail" for one night and had been raped by a bigger, stronger inmate.*

*The young man's shame at not being able to prevent the rape, coupled with his anger at the tremendous violation of his personhood, resulted in his withdrawing from normal social relationships with young women his own age, which increased his masturbation behavior. He avoided going to church, which had been a very positive experience for him prior to the rape.*

*Although he was not ready to accept his innocence, after a period of time he was prayerfully able to accept God's grace and forgive himself for his powerlessness and inability to prevent the rape. He was able to "reconnect" with the real God who genuinely loved him. After a short time, he accepted a meaningful position with a Christian agency, eliminated most of his masturbating, and was able to resume dating in a way that was appropriate for a young man of his age.*

Most people carry a collection of facts, reasons, and behaviors (of themselves or others) that have preceded their feelings and are often seen as the cause of their feelings. When listening to the surface reasons that are first presented, it is important to develop additional counseling skills. These skills assist you to "probe" for specific instances of helping, aggression, neglect, caring, nurturing, sensuality, indifference, prejudice, hurting, healing, accepting, abandoning, suffering, etc., that the person may need to get out in the open.

See chapter 5 for additional information about using prompts and probes.

---

**Skill Builder 3.4**  Think about what facts or feelings might lie under the surface of the following client statements if you were to probe them a little further.

**EXAMPLE**

*Client:* "Most of my marriage is OK, I guess."
*Possible Fact:* Client's marriage is not very satisfactory.
*Possible Feeling:* Client is unhappy.

**PRACTICE**

A. *Client:* "I think I will graduate from high school."

Possible Fact: _____

_____

Possible Feeling: _____

_____

B. *Client:* "On my job it never rains; it pours."

Possible Fact: _____

_____

Possible Feeling: _____

_____

---

## Third Level: Deep Searching for Values

*Following a seminar on Christian Approaches to Understanding Personality conducted at a large church in a rural area, people were invited to come to a smaller session for "positive personality testing." One woman came for testing but really wanted counseling. She took my associate (a woman) aside and shared that she was in her third marriage and was becoming very frightened. Her first husband had abused her, giving her a concussion. Her second husband also had physically abused her. Now her third husband was verbally abusing her, and she was frightened that the abuse would become physical.*

*Obviously, this lady needed some good pastoral counseling. Since we were located several hours away from the church, it would have been impractical for her to come see either of us for counseling on a regular basis. We inquired with the church pastor, who himself did not do counseling, if there was a trained Christian professional counselor in the area. He said that he was not aware of one but would try to help this lady.*

*While strongly encouraging her to seek local help and to keep her pastor informed of the circumstances within the marriage, my associate and I individually spent an hour or so with her before leaving the church.*

*During this time the Holy Spirit brought to my mind some research I had read about prisoners who had been convicted of violent crimes. The research suggested that these prisoners responded to people who were as far away from them as seventeen feet as "invading their space." One intriguing facet of the research was that they did not feel this fear and anger for someone whom they loved if the person was next to them and touching them in some loving way.*

*As an experiment, we suggested this woman approach her husband when he began to look or sound angry, stand right next to him, and place a hand around his waist in a loving way. We certainly did not suggest that this should be done in place of their going to an appropriate marriage counselor.*

*Three weeks later she called our office to announce that the "therapy" that we had "prescribed" was working! Every time her husband began to appear to be angry or agitated, she simply stood next to him and put her arm around his waist while he calmed down! However, (and this is often the problem with homework assignments) her next question was how long she needed to continue this course of action. Although it worked, she really did not like having to take responsibility for his calming down when he was acting in an immature and angry fashion toward her!*

*The client's "problem" was a misbelief (false value) that her life was not significant unless she was being yelled at or being physically hurt. Of course, she did not like being hurt, but she did not know how to be comfortable with a life that did not have this level of intensity.*

Often feelings that are attributed to particular reasons or "causes" are tied less to the facts that anchor them than to the belief systems by which those facts are interpreted. This can be true in terms of a client's attributing good or bad feelings to his or her own actions. It is even more frequently true when a client attributes his or her good or bad feelings to the actions of others. In a very real sense, behavior is translated by personal belief (values) into feelings, so that a change in a belief (value) may make as much or more difference in the feeling as a change in the behavior that seems to cause the feeling.

---

**Chart 3.1**

## BEHAVIOR is translated by BELIEF (or misbelief) into FEELING

---

An individual's beliefs (true values) or misbeliefs (false values) may originate in his or her family values, cultural acceptance, church traditions, scriptural knowledge, positive spiritual experiences with God, negative spiritual experiences with Satan, positive or negative life experiences, experience with

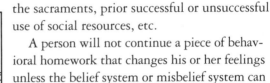

the sacraments, prior successful or unsuccessful use of social resources, etc.

A person will not continue a piece of behavioral homework that changes his or her feelings unless the belief system or misbelief system can also be changed in a congruent fashion.

This is why we cannot truly heal the brokenhearted simply by empathizing with their feelings or even by changing some portion of their behavior. The broken heart that is without hope for a worthwhile personal future, without faith in God, or without love from and for others is not going to be repaired by some simple piece of behavior homework.

We must be careful not to reduce the gospel message to a psychology that is devoid of spiritual power and principle. Truly transformational counseling must go beyond mere emotions. In speaking to pastoral counselors, Leanne Payne reminds us, "Thinking only of the person's emotional needs and the current wisdom for meeting them, the modern minister forgets to invoke the presence of God and call down upon the needy person the grace to repent. He has neglected the root healing, out of which all ongoing progress comes. The essential will in the needy person is left untouched, and he will be unable to stand." She continues, "To be a Christian minister is to call the needy to a radical and full repentance, and then, in the power of the Spirit to proclaim forgiveness in such a way that the repentant one can receive it. The Christian minister is a sacramental channel through which God's forgiveness flows."

The counselor's initial problem above was the failure to become partners with the client in the painful task of examining the misbelief system to determine what distorted values were causing her to select and marry dramatically abusive partners and to help her find biblical values (beliefs) that would lead to better choices.

See chapters 7 and 8 to learn specialty skills for the use of Scripture and prayer in the counseling process.

**Skill Builder 3.5** Behaviors are often translated by a person's beliefs or misbeliefs into feelings. Explore this connection by doing the following exercises.

EXAMPLE
*Behavior:* Smoked pot  *Belief:* Smoking pot is cool.  *Feeling:* Good about self
*Behavior:* Smoked pot  *Belief:* Smoking pot is sinful.  *Feeling:* Bad/guilty

PRACTICE

A. *Behavior:* Returned excess change received at supermarket

*Belief:* _____

_____

*Feeling:* Felt virtuous and happy

B. *Behavior:* Returned excess change received at supermarket

*Belief:* _____

_____

*Feeling:* Felt stupid

C. *Behavior:* Read a chapter of the Bible

*Belief:* God gives us guidance through the Bible.

*Feeling:* _____

_____

D. *Behavior:* Read a chapter of the Bible

*Belief:* Bible reading is ignorant and superstitious.

*Feeling:* _____

_____

## "Too-Narrow" Approaches

*One of my most tragic memories involves a friend who dropped by my house to talk to me about a career change. I was facing some personal challenges of my own at the time, so I limited my openness to him; we discussed only the "rational" topics of how to conduct his job search and improve his economic circumstances. I listened to my spirit and ability, but not to the deep need of his spirit or the wise promptings of the Holy Spirit. Three days later my friend jumped off a highway bridge and killed himself. Perhaps if I had listened to the despair of his spirit, I would have conducted an "index of lethality" assessment, realized how close he was to suicide, and referred him for psychiatric medication while we looked together at the deep spiritual emptiness of his life.*

We cannot get "stuck" in one lone area if we are to meet the goal of helping the client to effectively deal with life.

If we allow the client to keep the interview on the level of reason alone, then the likely result of all our work will be a sterile, philosophical resolution, which is still emotionally and spiritually bankrupt. We have allowed the client, in his or her denial, to exclude critical areas from the counseling process.

Interventions that only emphasize positive faith as an antidote to negative emotion run the risk of creating a thin layer of external optimism, plastered over a deep layer of internal fragmentation. The danger is that the person is afraid to do adequate reality testing of potential decisions. This is due to the client's fear that his or her optimism will crack and that the real fragmentation will show through.

A focus on changing social or economic circumstances, while often necessary, is not sufficient if the areas of mind, body/emotions, and faith are neglected.

Also, if we follow the path of some professional counselors and focus only on body chemistry and emotion, the danger is that the results may appear to be initially satisfying to the client but could be based on selfish hedonism. Pleasure seeking as a single value eventually fails because it ignores interpersonal responsibilities, logical consequences, and spiritual realities.

Techniques that focus on integrating feelings and reason are better than single-focus approaches but could still result in despair and suicide if they are not subsequently integrated with hope and faith.

Some popular Christian-counseling approaches that attempt to combine logic and faith may have a certain appeal to us as mature Christians. These systems actually result in an increase in vision and a certain mental understanding of the Scriptures. However, they may not adequately concern themselves with impact on the person's interpersonal relationships or internal emotions.

## Focusing on the Big Goal

*One of my counseling failures occurred with a pastor who was a Valium addict after having strained his back and being given the drug as a painkiller. He found the drug to be such a good mood changer that he began making excuses to have the prescription repeatedly renewed. I visited his home to counsel him on the Valium addiction and failed to notice a lack of interaction with his wife and children. In addition, while visiting his church, I witnessed his inspiring worship and excellent preaching abilities in action. It never crossed my mind to discuss his negative relationships with his superiors and his denomination. Although I did "talk him off" the Valium, several years later he left his wife, children, and church and moved into more serious addiction. Obviously, this is not exactly a counseling success story.*

It is important to remember that our big goal is one of restoring the broken-hearted person to a whole life. Reason, faith, and emotion should fit so well together that the person is able to deal effectively with his or her social environment in a responsible, moral, and rewarding way.

As spiritual counselors, we are very concerned with skills and therapeutic approaches. We are always in prayer that emotion, reason, faith, and changes in circumstances will be combined in the client in such a way that a fully integrated person will be the result. In Acts 4:29-30 the disciples prayed for boldness, healing, and miracles in the name of Jesus. They received everything they prayed for! In the same manner, as spiritual counselors, we have the right and responsibility to pray for the people we work with and to invest our love in them so that they will become fully integrated believers. Their faith, reason, and emotional focus will respond in ways that are personally rewarding for them and for the people around them, thereby glorifying God!

---

**Skill Builder 3.6** One of the important aspects of counseling is to define a goal for the counseling process and keep the process moving toward that goal. Define a possible goal for each of the situations described below:

A. *Client:* "I am very depressed about the sexual frequency in our marriage. My husband seems to want sex all the time, and I would like to have a more comfortable, loving relationship without so much sex. What do you think we ought to do about this?"

*Possible Goal:* _____

_____

_____

_____

B. Client: "I am not quite sure what to do about my business partner, Harry. I think he is taking money from our petty cash and may be stealing supplies from the business as well. I don't know how to talk to him about this. What do you suggest I do?"

Possible Goal: _____

_____

_____

C. *Client:* "I think the thing that really bothers me the most is my prayer life. I try to pray, but it's like talking to the ceiling, so then I quit praying for days or maybe even a week or two because it seems so pointless. Then I go to church and hear about all the people having marvelous answers to prayer, and I wish I had experiences like theirs. They seem to be doing so well in their lives, and I seem to be doing so poorly in general. What do you think I should do about this?"

Possible Goal: _____

_____

_____

Now you are ready to conduct and record your next practice counseling interview. As you did before, ask a friend, another student, or a family member to work with you on this exercise. Remind the person that he or she should talk about something real (not role play!). The topic may be happy or sad, important or merely trivial, so long as it is real. If you are using the same person, he or she may wish to continue talking about the same thing that has been talked about in previous interviews. This is perfectly permissible. However, during this interview you will want to try to respond using the new information and drawing on the insights you have been building during chapter 3.

After ten to twenty minutes of interviewing, turn the tape recorder off and stop the interview. Then spend half an hour playing the tape back and making notes about what the client said and how you responded on the "Taped Interview Analysis" page.

Chapter Three **BACK TALK**

Please answer the following questions for this chapter:

1. What is the main point of this chapter? _____

_____

_____

_____

2. What was your favorite illustration/story in this chapter? Why?_____

_____

_____

_____

3. Describe a personal experience you have had as a counselor or counselee (formal or informal) that relates to the content of this chapter: _____

_____

_____

_____

4. What question(s) do you have after reading this chapter? _____

_____

_____

_____

5. What would you like to learn more about in the rest of this manual? ____

_____

_____

Chapter Three **TAPED INTERVIEW ANALYSIS**

Name: _____

Date: _____

Interview Number: _____

1. What was the client's presenting (initial) problem or opportunity?_____

_____

_____

2. What skills did you attempt to practice in this interview? Give one or more

examples: _____

_____

_____

3. What do you feel you did best in this interview? _____

_____

_____

4. What do you feel you need to improve upon based on this interview? ____

_____

_____

5. Describe any surprises, shifts in direction or content, or significant positive

or negative turning points in this interview: _____

_____

_____

6. How was the client thinking and/or feeling by the end of this interview? __

_____

_____

7. If this were an interview series, what do you think might happen in the next interview? _____

_____

_____

8. What did you learn most about the process of personal counseling from conducting this interview? _____

_____

_____

_____

Chapter Three **THE COUNSELOR'S LIBRARY**

Consider adding one or more of these books to your counseling library:

Crabb, Lawrence J., Jr. *Effective Biblical Counseling*. Grand Rapids: Zondervan, 1977.
> Dr. Larry Crabb's book is a classic in the Christian counseling field. Crabb takes Albert Ellis's secular Rational Emotive Therapy and transforms it into a tool for Christian counselors to bring glory to God.

Egan, Gerard. *The Skilled Helper*. Second Edition. Pacific Grove, Cal.: Brooks/Cole Publishing, 1982.
> Dr. Egan's book has become the standard introductory counseling-skills text for hundreds of secular and Christian graduate schools across the country. The fifth edition (1995) is even better than the second edition.

*New American Standard Bible*. Chicago: Moody Press, 1977.
> Based on the 1901 American Standard Version, the NASB incorporates more recent discoveries of early Hebrew and Greek textual sources and presents the text in a fresher, more current English usage.

Payne, Leanne. *The Healing Presence*. Wheaton, Ill.: Crossway Books, 1989.
> This is the centerpiece of a group of marvelous books by this author about the power of grace to change lives when sensitively and lovingly applied through healing prayer. A must-read for every pastoral counselor.

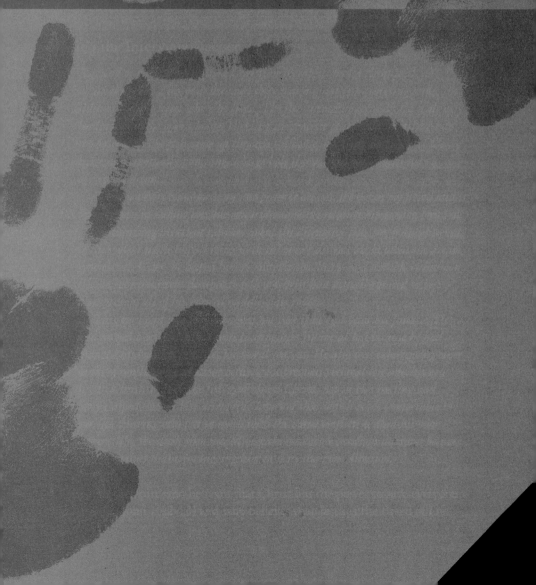

# PART TWO

# ADVANCED SKILLS

# Doc & Duck

LISTEN WELL

Doc & Duck © 1999 Andrew J. Cheydleur

# Advanced Listening Skills

LISTENING IS important, but merely listening without purpose would not be counseling. We have the ministry of reconciliation (2 Cor. 5:18-20). The question naturally follows, What should be reconciled? While it would be correct to say that our primary spiritual ministry is to reconcile people with God, it would not be sufficient. Much of the work of ministry is with people who already have accepted Christ but have other areas of their lives that are not yet balanced.

As we listen, reflect, and attempt to heal people through spiritual counseling, we are particularly concerned about the areas of their lives that are not reconciled with each other. The four primary areas that may be out of sync with one another are mind/content, body/emotions, spirit, and social environment.

## "Remarrying" Content and Emotion

*A friend of mine retired from the United States Navy after twenty years of service. He bought a motel and made enough money the first year to buy a new Cadillac, a dream purchase all of his life. He called me shortly after he made the purchase.*

*"I finally bought my new Cadillac this past week," he told me. I responded that he must be very happy about having been able to buy a Cadillac (trying, of course, to catch the emotion of the moment). My friend exclaimed, "No, I am not at all happy with the new Cadillac; the stupid speedometer cable snapped nineteen miles after I left the dealership! Now it's back in the shop until they put in a new cable!"*

*My friend is a healthy-minded believer who was able to own his own anger and frustration over the fact that his "symbol of perfection" turned out not to be so perfect after all. During our conversation he even gained enough perspective to be somewhat amused at the whole situation.*

If a man were to tell me, "I have just bought a new car," I would not automatically know whether he was happy, sad, or had mixed emotions about this new purchase. If my own prior experience with new automobiles was positive, I might assume he was happy. On the other hand, if I were thinking about the cost, I might assume he was regretful! It may be he already knows exactly how he feels and has simply not communicated those feelings to me, or he might not yet have sorted out his own feelings about this new purchase. In my friend's case, I assumed I knew his emotion, based on too limited content, and I missed his frustration.

Consider this skillful example of a client and counselor working well together to connect content and emotion:

> *Client:* "She tries to make me feel stupid!"
> *Counselor:* "And that really irritates you."
> *Client:* "It really does! She always has to be right!"
> *Counselor:* "So having her in your room is . . ."
> *Client:* "Irritating! Irritating!"

In this example the counselor is so "tuned in" to the client that it is almost like one person thinking aloud, and a clear perspective is rapidly developing. However, your clients will not always come with this kind of perspective, and you may not be able to clearly connect their emotions with the content. One of your tasks as a counselor is to help them do this.

Suppose a person talking to you about her job says:

> *Client:* "People at my office aren't very cooperative."

You might respond by saying:

> *You:* "It bothers you that the people at your office don't help you with your projects."

This type of response adds the implied emotion to the content of the client's first statement. When you are accurate in doing this, you help the client to own the emotion of which he or she may have been only partially aware.

Conversely, a client may come to you exclaiming:

> *Client:* "I'm so mad, I can't see straight!"

You might respond by reflecting only the emotion and not the content:

*You:* "You are really angry today."

As you are willing to accept the legitimacy of the client's anger, he or she may be free to discuss the source of the anger.

*Client:* "Yes, I think it's very unfair that my boss always gives the plum assignments to Shirley rather than to me!"

In this exchange the person is now able to "remarry" the emotion back into the content disclosure it triggered.

Although you would not always want to do it in a rigid, prescribed format, much of the task of the counselor may, in essence, be helping a person to restructure his or her thinking in terms of "you feel_____ (some emotion) because of_____ (some circumstance)." When you are able to help the person "remarry" content and emotion, you help him or her take a significant step toward owning and analyzing those emotions. This step often must precede significant work on the areas of spirit or social environment.

---

**⚡ Skill Builder 4.1**  In the following exercises, restate the client's communication so that the "content" is reconnected with the implied "emotion":

EXAMPLE

*Client:* "I had dinner all prepared, and my husband just called and said he would be home late from work."

*Restatement:* "You are disappointed that your careful preparation of supper will go to waste or have to be reheated because his job schedule is so hard to predict."

PRACTICE

A. *Client:* "My supervisor asked me to lie just so that she could get her boss in trouble!"

*Restatement:* _____

_____

_____

_____

B. *Client:* "I'm paying a mint to be in this cancer hospital. The food is lousy, and the nurses won't even smile at you."

*Restatement:* _____

_____

_____

_____

## Connecting Emotions and Values

Often, as you are exploring feelings or emotions with the person, you will begin to perceive the values and beliefs that lie in the area of the spirit and are connected to those emotions. In the previous example, the interview might at some point proceed to the level of "so the reason that you are so angry (emotion) is that you believe (the area of the spirit) that a boss should be fair (value) in the way he or she hands out assignments." In this example you have now captured how the emotion is tied to content, and you are beginning to explore more deeply how the emotion springs from a strongly held value, which is part of the client's belief system.

The following example is taken from an actual interview between a counselor-in-training and a college student from Puerto Rico. Note how well the counselor helps the client focus on her values:

(Middle of interview)

*Client:* "We're even losing the meaning of our celebrations—such as trading the 'Three Kings' for Santa Claus."

*Counselor:* "So keeping your culture intact, even though you're in this country, is important to you."

*Client:* "Yes! to keep our own things, and to let others share in our culture."

*Counselor:* "Uh huh . . ."

*Client:* "Some of the Hispanic students just look at the advantages here and do not want to return. It hurts—to know that they are denying their own island."

*Counselor:* "So the things they are looking for in this country are really materialistic-type things."

*Client:* "Yeah—and they consider being Hispanic kind of the lowest . . ."

As the interview continues, the counselor is able to help the client clarify the value conflict between pride in her own culture and wanting to be accepted by her peers. This clarification of value conflicts provides the perspective necessary to any meaningful decision making.

---

**Skill Builder 4.2** In the following exercises, restate the client's communication so that the emotion is reconnected with an implied value:

## EXAMPLE
*Client:* "I was incredibly angry that she would ask me to lie like that."
*Restatement:* "So your anger was even greater because the thing she wanted you to do violated your moral code, and you believe honesty is very important."

## PRACTICE
A. *Client:* "I feel very frustrated because my sister wants to bring her three kids and move in with me and my husband. We only have a little house."

*Restatement:* _____

_____

_____

B. *Client:* "I just can't stop crying and accusing myself. I didn't realize our puppy had gotten big enough to jump the garden fence, and now he's been hit by a truck!"

*Restatement:* _____

_____

_____

## Action to Alter Circumstances

In the workplace example, one thing that was not considered by the client or the counselor was any external circumstances that may have influenced how the boss distributed assignments. They did not consider whether or how these circumstances (the social environment) could be altered by the client in order to change the situation. In an extended counseling process, we begin with discovering preexisting content, emotions, and values. As we explore the value conflicts that surface, we are able to help clients come to some kind of new perspective. The new perspective opens the possibility for appropriate decision making.

Once a decision has been reached about what clients want to have happen, then we can help them brainstorm to find one or more action plans. This will help them alter the circumstances and social environment in a positive and effective way. Then, when the actions have actually taken place, we help the clients into relationships of accountability with a second person or a small group that can support them in continuing the effective action plan.

In order for people to be completely reconciled, each area (mind, body/emotions, spirit, social environment) must be given attention during the counseling process.

It is important that the counselor not try to "force" the counseling process into decisions, action plans, and accountability too soon. A major part of the work of most counseling is in the first two areas: discovery and defining new perspectives.

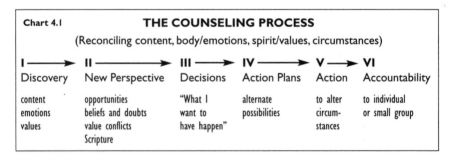

| Chart 4.1 | **THE COUNSELING PROCESS** | | | | |
|---|---|---|---|---|---|
| | (Reconciling content, body/emotions, spirit/values, circumstances) | | | | |
| I ⟶ | II ⟶ | III ⟶ | IV ⟶ | V ⟶ | VI |
| Discovery | New Perspective | Decisions | Action Plans | Action | Accountability |
| content | opportunities | "What I | alternate | to alter | to individual |
| emotions | beliefs and doubts | want to | possibilities | circum- | or small group |
| values | value conflicts | have happen" | | stances | |
| | Scripture | | | | |

This means that over and over again, the counselor must focus intense energy on attending to the discrepancies between content statements and emotion statements. The counselor helps the client to "pull them together" until he or she is honest about feelings and can identify the values and beliefs to which the feeling is actually connected.

✋ **Skill Builder 4.3** In the following examples, suggest one or more possible options that the client could explore to "alter the circumstances" of a situation:

EXAMPLE

*Client:* "I know I can be an effective addictions counselor because I've helped a lot of my friends get sober. But every time I apply for a counseling job, I get beaten out by somebody who has a degree in counseling or a CAC credential!"

*Options Statement:* "So it looks like, to change this situation, you are going to have to go back to school, either to get a counseling degree or a CAC credential."

PRACTICE

A. *Client:* "I've already graduated from Bible college, and I want to spend all of my time loving people into the kingdom, but everybody says I'm a boring preacher, so I keep getting turned down for jobs as a church pastor."

*Options Statement:* _____

_____

_____

B. *Client:* "My husband confessed that he cheated on me sexually when he was at the sales convention in New York. I think I really have forgiven him, but now I'm worried that he or I might have AIDS. The terror of it keeps me awake many nights!"

*Options Statement:* _____

_____

_____

For more information about decision making and action planning, see chapter 9.

## Seven Reasons Feelings Don't Track

> One of my counseling students told this story about a friend in high school: "There was a girl in my class who was a total wreck. She was up one minute and down the next. Her emotions were always out of whack. When she was put on medication, she was fine. In fact, she was almost like a new person—fun to be with and in control of herself. She later confided that she had some kind of chemical disturbance and that she was now taking medicine and was feeling a lot better."

There are a number of reasons why a person's feelings may not accurately match his or her circumstances. A major reason a client may have feelings that don't seem to track with the circumstances or may discuss circumstances without being in touch with any deep feelings could be a prior history of sexual, physical, or emotional **victimization**. Research suggests there may be as many as one in four adult women who were sexually molested as children. The number of men may be as high as one in every eight adult men. Often adults who have been sexually molested, physically abused, or emotionally abandoned as children become afraid to own their own emotions when they are being "revictimized" in some way as adults.

The second reason feelings don't track, or don't show, is that a person who is being socially oppressed or treated unfairly on the job but who is not able to articulate his or her anger may turn that anger inward in the form of **depression**. In "keeping a lid" on anger, he or she may have to use a great deal of energy. This caps off the person's anger but prevents him or her from experiencing positive emotions of joy and happiness even when off the job and in a positive home or social setting. The counselor will have to be very sensitive and empathetic in order for the person to be able to break through that bottleneck and own the fact that he or she does feel badly about what is happening on the job.

If you are counseling a depressed client, it is important that some of your counseling sessions be done in a sufficiently private setting, so it will be "safe" for the person to begin releasing that anger. Once it is released, it may be displayed in quite a quite dramatic fashion, so be prepared to accept the anger when it surfaces and acknowledge it rather than block it. It could be more difficult for the person to get in touch with positive emotions later if you become frightened and try to block the negative emotions now.

Of course, depression can be caused by many factors, including a prior history of victimization, distorted brain chemistry, etc. A sufficiently deep hurt in adulthood can also bring about depression even if there was no problem in childhood.

Besides victimization and depression, a third factor that can prevent the client from being accurately connected to emotion and content may be a current experience of **spiritual warfare**. This may take the form of oppression from without or temptation from within. The spiritual and psychological energy a person draws on for these battles can drain that person physically. It can make it almost impossible for the person to respond with creative joy to the potentials and opportunities in his or her environment. The oppression or temptation, and the agony of its battle, is acknowledged and dealt with in spiritual counseling. Then the person may be able to gain enough strength to be successful in fighting it or to move ahead in any other areas of his/her life.

A fourth factor that sometimes makes it difficult for a person to clearly connect content, emotion, and values may be the area of **unconfessed sin.** This can either be the sin of the individual or sin in his or her immediate social environment.

> *Dr. Anna Terruwe, M.D., in her book* Healing the Unaffirmed, *discusses the case of a man with low self-esteem whose father had refused to acknowledge that his own father had been an American Indian. Due to the racial prejudice of the community, the grandfather was not allowed to be buried in the community graveyard! The father's repudiation of his heritage and the community's sin of racial prejudice were discovered; both needed to be acknowledged. Then the man in treatment was able to deal with the sin, forgive his father, acknowledge his grandfather's heritage, and have faith to move ahead in terms of his own development of self-esteem.*

Of course, unconfessed personal sin may have much the same effect on faith and self-esteem. It is usually easier for the counselor and client to discover this kind of connection and resolve it through the person's accepting forgiveness.

The fifth reason that may make connecting emotions and content difficult is a **lack of trust in the counselor** or counseling process by the client. This may not have anything personally to do with the client's attitude toward you as a counselor. This lack of trust may be because it is too early in the counseling process or because the client doesn't see you as a person having credibility. He or she may have had previous negative experiences in trusting other people, or he or she may feel that the counseling interview is moving along too rapidly.

You and I would not want to share our deepest and most frightening secrets with someone else unless we had very carefully built up a pattern of trust and dependability with that individual. There is no reason we should expect our clients to be able to move rapidly into trust in all areas of their lives, even if they have already trusted us with some of the smaller things.

Of course, a sixth factor that may affect a person's ability to connect cognitive and emotional material is the area of **brain chemistry disturbance.** Sometimes the taking of an appropriate stabilizing drug, such as lithium, may make all the difference in a person's being able to function on an even keel, because his or her brain simply does not work properly without the stabilizing chemical. In addition, persons in early recovery from using illegal mood-changing drugs such as heroin or cocaine may have residual brain-chemistry effects for a period of time after stopping their use. This means that some areas of memory, thinking, and emotion will not connect together appropriately until the brain has had enough time to do some internal repair work. In such cases problems in connecting content and emotion should not be attributed to spiritual or psychological resistance on the part of the client, nor to lack of skill on the part of the counselor, but should simply be accepted as part of the difficulty in healing following such abuse of the body's chemistry.

Although it is not too frequent (depending on geography and sub-culture), consideration should also be given to a seventh factor: the possibility that a client's problems in connecting emotions and values with appropriate content may be due to thought disturbances with an origin in **occult experiences** or practices. (See chapter 9, "Speciality Intervention Skills.")

When occult practices are imposed on young children, there can be severe personality disturbances in adult life. For adults who have merely dabbled in these areas, there may still be some emotional carryover, which can be effectively dealt with through counseling and simple deliverance prayer.

---

**Skill Builder 4.4**  Give examples of the seven possible causes to listen for in counseling when your client's feelings and/or values do not "track" or when they seem to be inappropriate for the circumstances or situation the client is discussing.

A. _____

_____

B. _____

_____

C. _____

_____

D. _____

_____

E. _____

_____

F. _____

_____

G. _____

_____

## Teaching and Comforting

Scripture states that we are to "teach and comfort each other" (1 Thess. 5:9-11). In the counseling process, we allow the clients to teach us about themselves. We respond to them by reflecting back what we are learning in a more focused and connected way. This brings both clarity and comfort to the clients.

As you practice the Skill Builders in this chapter, focus your attention on trying to see the potential connections, sometimes clearly evident and sometimes rather veiled, in the client's communication.

Next, prepare to conduct and tape-record your next practice recording interview. You may ask a friend, family member, or another student to be the "client" for this interview, and you will, as before, ask him or her to talk about something real, not to role-play an imaginary situation.

For this ten-to-twenty-minute interview, ask your "client" to discuss something painful, confusing, or both. Listen especially for connections between content and emotion, and emotion and values. Risk "filling in the gaps" when these are not clearly stated, and if possible, complete this session by summarizing the action options for altering the circumstances that you and the client have explored during the interview.

After you complete this interview, listen to the tape and make specific notes for yourself regarding:

• connections between content and emotion;
• connections between emotion and values; and
• action plans (options) to alter circumstances.

Remember to give your "time signals" at the beginning of the interview, five minutes before the end, and at the end of the interview.

In your notes be clear about what the client has said and about connections you have effectively restated, or failed to restate effectively, during the counseling process. Also, give yourself special extra credit for any jumps of personal intuition or Holy Spirit revelations that you have stated and that the client has positively received.

Complete the "Taped Interview Analysis" form for this interview.

Chapter Four  **BACK TALK**

Please answer the following questions for this chapter:

1. What is the main point of this chapter? _____

_____

_____

_____

_____

2. What was your favorite illustration/story in this chapter? Why?_____

_____

_____

_____

_____

3. Describe a personal experience you have had as a counselor or counselee (formal or informal) that relates to the content of this chapter: _____

_____

_____

_____

_____

4. What question(s) do you have after reading this chapter?_____

_____

_____

_____

_____

5. What would you like to learn more about in this book? _____

_____

_____

_____

_____

Chapter Four **TAPED INTERVIEW ANALYSIS**

Name: _____

Date: _____

Interview Number: _____

1. What was the client's presenting (initial) problem or opportunity?_____

_____

_____

_____

2. What skills did you attempt to practice in this interview? Give one or more

examples: _____

_____

_____

_____

3. What do you feel you did best in this interview? _____

_____

_____

_____

4. What do you feel you need to improve upon based on this interview? ___

_____

_____

_____

5. Describe any surprises, shifts in direction or content, or significant positive

or negative turning points in this interview: _____

_____

_____

_____

6. How was the client thinking and/or feeling by the end of this interview? ___

_____

_____

_____

_____

7. If this were an interview series, what do you think might happen in the next interview?_____

_____

_____

_____

_____

8. What did you learn most about the process of personal counseling from conducting this interview? _____

_____

_____

_____

_____

Chapter Four **THE COUNSELOR'S LIBRARY**

Consider adding one or more of these books to your counseling library:

Lucado, Max. *He Still Moves Stones.* Dallas: Word Publishing, 1993.
> Max Lucado wakes us up to the present-tense interventions of a "never-say-die Galilean who majors in stepping in when everyone else steps out," with tenderness enough to give to all kinds of hurting people.

Narramore, Clyde M. *The Psychology of Counseling.* Grand Rapids: Zondervan, 1974.
> First published in 1960, Dr. Narramore's classic introduced professional counseling to the evangelical ministry with wide acceptance.

Sandford, John, and Paula Sandford. *Healing the Wounded Spirit.* South Plainfied, N.J.: Bridge Publishing, 1985.
> This is a very frank and open book about topics often hidden, including rejection and child abuse among Christians, generational sin, and wounds stemming from occult practices. Hundreds of examples of helpful, healing interventions are given.

Terruwe, Anna A., and Conrad W. Baars. *Healing the Unaffirmed.* New York: Alba House, 1976.
> A professional account of healings from childhood deprivation neurosis through counseling saturated with love. It will awaken your sensitivity to those who are deeply hurt yet are not mentally ill.

# Doc & Duck

# Advanced Challenging Skills

*"So you really feel she was unfair and discriminatory to you, and you were angry because a teacher shouldn't be that way." (empathy reflection)*

*"Have you experienced anything like that before from a person in authority over you?" (probe)*

WHILE EMPATHY skills are critical to faith-based counseling, empathy is only part of counseling. The book of Proverbs reminds us that we are not only to comfort each other but are to sharpen each other as iron sharpens iron (Prov. 27:17). The way in which this occurs during the counseling process is through the skillful use of probes, prompts, questions, and acoustical mirrors. These are not used with the purpose of making the client uncomfortable; nor are they used simply to gather information. The two purposes of these somewhat intrusive techniques are to clarify the client's values and value conflicts and clearly define the problem situations with which the client is dealing.

## Using Prompts and Probes

*Prompts* are useful in helping passive people tell their stories:

"Tell me more. . . ."
"Please go on. . . ."
"And then . . ."

*Probes* help keep more active clients focused on the relevant and important issues, leading up to decision making and problem resolution:

"Could you give me an example?"

"How does that compare with what you said before?"

"How did she respond when you told her that?"

Prompts and probes may be focused to help a client identify specific experiences, behaviors, or feelings. This provides a more concrete picture of what is actually going on. It enables the counselor to more accurately connect content and emotions with the client's values and social environment, which is preparation for decision making and action planning.

## Probing and Prompting Effectively

Probes and prompts are usually most effective and least threatening when they are phrased in the form of sentences rather than questions. As Gerard Egan points out in his excellent book *The Skilled Helper,* "Statements are gentler forms of probes than questions." Since all probes are somewhat intrusive, they serve as challenges to the client, so the more gentle sentence format usually creates less defensiveness:

"Why don't you think they were fair to you?" [question probe]

"So you don't think they were fair to you. . . ." [sentence probe]

Also, the counselor should not overly depend on strong probes, especially in the early stages of the interview. However, gentle prompts such as "Tell me a little more about that" or "Give me an example" can be very effective in moving an interview along or helping it to become more concrete. Generally, it is more helpful if the counselor avoids using interpretive questions like "Why?" or "What did you mean by that?" and questions that can be answered by a simple yes or no. If questions are used at all, it is best that they be open-ended, information-seeking questions such as "What sort of feelings did you have when that occurred?"

✊ **Skill Builder 5.1**   Practice selecting and using question probes/prompts for the following exercises:

EXAMPLE

*Client:* "It seems I always have bad luck in restaurants when I eat out!"

*Probe/Prompt:* "Could you give me an example?"

PRACTICE

A. *Client:* "And then she backed up, clear across the parking lot, and rammed right into my fender!"

*Probe/Prompt:* _____

_____

_____

B. *Client:* "Last night he confessed he had been dating my best friend behind my back and had even bought her flowers last Saturday."

*Probe/Prompt:* _____

_____

_____

One of the reasons probes and prompts are so important is that they help move the client beyond his or her own point of view. In the early stages of counseling, extensive use of empathy is made in order to explore the client's own point of view, but in the later stages of counseling, we want to broaden the client's perspective and open up other options for decision making.

## Counselor Assertiveness

Some beginning pastoral counselors are drawn to the ministry of counseling because they are "nice people." They want to express love and gentleness to others, and they find that the development of empathy skills within counseling comes to them rather naturally. The ability to appropriately use prompts and probes seems to be much more difficult.

Even using a simple prompt such as "And then . . ." or employing a low-level content probe such as "What did you do next?" may be difficult for some timid counselors.

If you are one of these people, you will want to hold on to the promise that God does give strength to us in all that we have to do (Ps. 29:11).

Practice some of the following exercises developed by Sheila Fabricant and the Linn Brothers (*Prayer Course for Healing Life's Hurts*):

*Take someone with whom you need to be lovingly honest out to dinner. Spend the time really loving and enjoying that person. If honest confrontations come naturally from your deepest love for the person, try to express your feelings.*

*Read John 2:13-25, where Jesus sees injustice and cleanses the temple. Ask Jesus to show you one situation that needs to be changed, e.g., a child needing attention, a lonely neighbor, an upcoming legislative bill that needs a letter to Congress, a way in which you or another are being treated unjustly. Feel Jesus' anger at seeing someone being hurt. Then let Jesus show you what He would do to correct the situation, and take the first step in what He wants you to do about it.*

*Spend the day really trying to listen and enjoy a person whom you find difficult to love, and you may just find that the longer you spend with that person, the easier it becomes to change your attitude.*

At this point you may be asking how you decide when to be assertive and forward and when to just listen. Remember, you never "just listen" but always respond by reflecting content or emotion—even at the beginning. Then use prompts to keep the interview moving, and probes to shift it to a deeper level (such as emotions or values) or keep it on focus.

In using prompts and probes, it's important to remember that counseling is not simply a polite conversation. It is not rude for you to interrupt the client and say, "I don't think I quite understand what you have just said. Could you be a little more specific?" or "It might help if you could back up and tell me exactly what you did in that situation." As the counselor, your use of probes and prompts is not inappropriate even when it is intrusive, so long as the goal is to help the client to become more specific and to clarify what he or she has experienced, how he or she feels, or what he or she believes.

**Skill Builder 5.2** Use a sentence probe to interrupt the client and clarify what is meant in the following exercises. Reminder: Avoid using probe questions that can be answered by a simple yes or no, and avoid using questions that begin with the word *why*. In these two exercises, try using sentence (not question) probes.

## EXAMPLE

*Client:* "He's probably the best pastor and the worst husband in the world. I love the public attention we're getting, but I can't stand living with him at home anymore!"

*Sentence Probe:* "There seems to be a sort of contradiction here . . . maybe a Jekyll-and-Hyde thing or something. Maybe you could give me a couple of concrete examples so that I can understand this a little better."

## PRACTICE

A. *Client:* "I'm tired of traveling and selling all the time—it used to be fun, but I just dread it every time I climb in the airplane or get in the car to go to a new city."

*Sentence Probe:* _____

_____

_____

B. *Client:* "My grades are still pretty good, at least in most of my subjects, but I find myself bored, looking out the window and daydreaming, wondering if I should be doing something for God now instead of wasting all this time in school."

*Sentence Probe:* _____

_____

_____

## Providing Strength and Security

> *"That last comment seemed to go around in circles; could we take this apart into a couple of distinct pieces?"*

As a counselor, you need to be secure enough that asking a client a direct question for clarification does not make you feel as if you are looking stupid. A question should simply be an honest expression of the need for understanding that must take place in the counseling relationship.

As believers, we want to know that God is strong (Ps. 8:2; 18:2; 37:39). As such, our clients do not expect us to be wimpy within the counseling process. You may say to a client, "Well, what are some of the tough questions you need to ask yourself in order to work this out?" You are doing one of the things the client wants you to do, which is to help him or her face his or her problems. It might be irresponsible and uncaring to raise such a question in the first few minutes of the initial interview; it would be equally irresponsible never to raise such a question in the midst of difficult issues you are exploring with a client over a period of time.

In Psalm 18:1 the author responds to God by saying, "I will love you, O Lord, my strength." It is the strength and dependability of God that frees the psalmist for the emotion of love. In a similar way, the client is free to explore difficult and fragile emotions and values when he or she perceives the counselor as a source of strength.

Actually, the client might have thought the response went around in circles too, and may genuinely welcome the opportunity to revisit the material, slow down, and consider it from several careful and more reasonable perspectives.

---

**Skill Builder 5.3**   Use a "direct request for clarification" in the following exercises:

EXAMPLE

*Client:* "I'm so mad at Sheila, I can't see straight! I just want to pull her hair out by the roots or hurt her bad for what she did to me!"
*Request for Clarification:* "So you are really angry at her! Exactly what did she do that made you so mad?"

PRACTICE

A. *Client:* "Ever since Edward and I broke up, I've been depressed and thinking of killing myself. And lately, I think I'm getting up the courage to do it."

*Direct Request for Clarification:* _____

_____

_____

_____

B. *Client:* "If it weren't for my mother, I never would have gone to medical school, so I guess I should be grateful—at least, she tells me I should be. She still controls my life in so many ways that I find it offensive and even humiliating."

*Direct Request for Clarification:* _____

_____

_____

_____

## Using Small Probes and Prompts

Sometimes, as counselors, we keep the interview focused by using small probes such as:

"You were not completely happy?"
"So you are actually exhausted?"

Other minimal prompts may be simple, one-word exclamations such as:

"Uh-huh . . . "
"Mmm . . . "
"Yes . . . "
"I see. . . . "
"Oh . . . "

Nonverbal prompts include such basic gestures as nodding your head yes or moving forward in your chair.

Some beginning counselors become frightened. They want to retreat into side issues when their probes or prompts begin to expose weak, sinful, or broken areas in the lives of their clients, especially if anguish or anger is expressed. Instead of being afraid of such revelations, we need to stand on the promises of God's Word, which proclaims, "The Lord upholds all who fall" (Ps. 145:14) and "Though he fall, he shall not be utterly cast down, for the Lord upholds him with His hand" (Ps. 37:24). Our ultimate purpose in counseling is to restore strength to the person who is weak or stumbling and/or suffering from social oppression and brokenness. We define our purpose not in covering up for clients or even in exposing them but in *healing* them: "Those who stumbled are girded with strength" (1 Sam. 2:4), knowing that "[His] strength is made perfect in weakness" (2 Cor. 12:9).

We often may feel we could say a lot more or respond with some sort of either condemnation or rescue attempts to the painful and intimate revelations clients make. However, these minimal probes may be far more effective (although they do require some spiritual discipline on our part) than a more extended preaching or comforting.

The spiritual disciplines of the counselor such as bearing, believing, hoping, and enduring (1 Cor. 13:7), used within the counseling process, really make the difference between amateur and professional counseling. They also make the difference between counseling that is Spirit led and counseling that only comes out of our human spirit, ideas, and experiences.

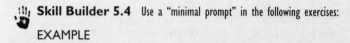

**Skill Builder 5.4** Use a "minimal prompt" in the following exercises:

EXAMPLE

*Client:* "Well, it seems to be a pretty good job so far, but I've only been there three weeks, and there are a few things that bug me already."
*Minimal Prompt:* "Things that bug you?"

PRACTICE

A. *Client:* "You know, I went down front at the crusade last week, and I think I really got born again this time—at least something good happened there."

*Minimal Prompt:* _____

_____

B. *Client:* "There we were, just two good ol' boys, sitting in the car outside the bar and talking about life and philosophy and all that stuff for, oh, maybe four hours."

*Minimal Prompt:* _____

_____

## Wounding and Healing

Frank Damazio (*The Making of a Leader*) recommends these preparations for your own spirit:

- *Be healed (yourself) and free of a wounded spirit.*
- *Have the people at heart, which is the heart of God.*
- *Remember (your) miserable condition before God healed (your) own wounds, lest (you) become impatient and angry with people.*
- *Have a large heart that identifies with the wounded and brokenhearted.*

Nobody likes to be wounded. When we use probes and prompts in counseling, we may worry that we are wounding the client, when what we are actually doing is emotional surgery. We are penetrating into the unhealed, sensitive baggage that the client may have been carrying around for years. We all know that a person may be hurt by gossip (Prov. 18:14) or by another person's liberty, which is offensive to his or her own current state of faith (1 Cor. 8:12-13). Some clients may actually have wounds that come from unconfessed sin and may feel God has hurt them rather than placing the responsibility on themselves (Pss. 69:26; 64:7). When we are in the process of prompting and probing, we may inadvertently open some of these wounds and cause new ones (Prov. 27:6). But our purpose is to heal, not to hurt.

Any time you are in doubt about a specific probe or prompt, you should clearly listen to your own spirit as well as to the Spirit of God. Ascertain the purpose of the prompt, probe, or value reflection you are considering. Your purpose may be cloudy or related to your own unhealed wounds or anger. If so, stay with reflecting the client's content and feelings until you have had an opportunity to resolve any issues between you and the Lord. With Jesus, our purpose must always be to "heal the brokenhearted" (Isa. 61:1; Hos. 6:1; Luke 10:34).

## Combining Empathy and Probes

> Counselor: *"I can see that you believe that the school's grading policy is very unfair. Maybe you could give me a couple of examples of people who got different grades for work of similar quality."*

One of the ways we keep our probes in the service of healing rather than hurting is to continually combine them with empathy. Just as God's purpose is to give rest to us (Heb. 4:9), our purpose is to bring peace to the mind and spirit of the client. For example, the preceding response combines empathy with a probe. This type of probe requires the client to be accurate

and honest with himself and the counselor rather than indulging in a generalized polemic about the school. When the empathy is placed before the probe, it is much easier for the client to accept.

Take a look at the following example of a sentence probe without an empathy statement:

> Counselor: "I still don't understand why he makes you so angry."

This *could* lead to a client being specific, but it is more likely that the client will merely feel misunderstood and perhaps negatively challenged. A better use of this probe would be:

> Counselor: "It seems as though every time he walks into your office, your blood pressure rises! He obviously has some way of getting your goat, but I haven't exactly figured out what it is at this point."

That kind of empathy/probe combination allows the client to become specific about what the "oppressor" is doing. The client does not feel that the counselor has somehow taken the other side or has simply missed the pain, fear, and confusion that the client is subjectively experiencing.

 **Skill Builder 5.5** Practice combining empathy with your probe in the following exercises:

EXAMPLE

*Client:* "It may not be all that Christian, but they are lying about me in public. I want to hire the biggest, meanest attorney in town and squash them like bugs!"
*Empathy/Probe:* "So you are angry about how unfairly you are being treated and want somebody powerful enough to cut them down to size. Have you thought of any other ways to respond to this problem?"

PRACTICE

A. *Client:* "Some of the people at my seminary believe it is possible for people to marry against God's will, so the marriage is not really scripturally valid. I think my marriage might be like that."

*Empathy/Probe:* _____

_____

_____

B. *Client:* "This is ridiculous! He just went out and bought a new car for himself—which I wanted him to do, and we can afford the payments—but he also bought a stupid guarantee for an extra eight hundred dollars, so we can't pay the rent and food this month!"

*Empathy/Probe:* _____

_____

_____

## Prompting New Ideas

> Counselor: *"You know the Bible says he who trusts in the Lord will prosper (Prov. 28:25); what are some things for which God seems to be prompting you to trust Him?"*

In the latter stages of the counseling process, prompts and probes are often used to help people explore alternate possibilities. Prompts and probes are also used to help flesh out goals and possible programs to fulfill them. For a healthy and creative person, this process almost becomes a fulfillment of John 15:11, demonstrating that we can be full of God's joy. For a sad, depressed, or alienated client, we should expect there will be specific problems in this creative process, so our prompts and probes will still need to be tentative, and we will need to express a great deal of empathy during the process.

Confidence is one of the ingredients of creativity, but clients often have fear, which saps creative energy. Where creative people often accept ambigu-

ity, the client under stress may have fixed, self-defeating habits. These may be very difficult to admit. Creativity requires a certain level of independence. Some clients may be very dependent on us and/ or on other authority figures in their lives. These clients may be unwilling to provide any answers unless they can feel they are "approved" before they provide them.

In the development of alternate action plans and other kinds of creative tasks, a certain amount of nonconformity is useful. However, clients may either be extreme conformists or have some pathological nonconformity, such as drug abuse or violence, in their past, making them hesitant to become nonconforming even in the search for a positive future goal.

For clients who are believers, it is sometimes helpful to combine a prompt with an appropriate Scripture, thus providing security while at the same time encouraging creativity.

**Skill Builder 5.6** In the following exercises, practice combining your probe/prompt with Scripture to create security and/or confidence:

EXAMPLE

*Client:* "She wants us to get married and have babies right away, but I'm still not absolutely sure she's the right girl for me for a lifetime."

*Scripture/Probe:* "Proverbs 11:14 teaches us there is safety in many counselors. Whom could you get feedback from who knows both of you?"

PRACTICE

A. *Client:* "On the surface, my new boss and I have similar backgrounds, but I'm beginning to think our values are miles apart; some days I'm not even sure she's a Christian at all."

*Scripture/Probe:* _____

_____

_____

B. *Client:* "My husband ran off and divorced me three years ago to marry his secretary. I didn't think I would ever want to marry again, but I must admit I'm somewhat attracted to the new choir director at my church, who is single and has never been married."

*Scripture/Probe:* _____

_____

_____

## Other Forms of Prompts

Also, such written prompts as personal journals, activity logs, and checklists may help a person to move into creative action planning while still preserving the security of a predetermined structure.

Don't limit yourself to the examples given in this chapter. Create your own unique prompts and probes; experiment with the process of challenging. Then, as you do your own recorded interview, practice using prompts and probes within the process of the interview, and listen to your own level of comfort or lack of comfort during this practice.

Prepare to conduct and tape-record your next practice interview after completing the Skill Builders.

In this thirty-to-forty-five-minute interview, continue to practice your listening, reflection and empathy skills (including use of the "empathy-sandwich" technique). Also, practice listening to and making practical use of the "nudges" and "hunches" you receive from the Holy Spirit.

In addition, continue to strengthen your ability to reconnect content to emotion, emotion to values, and values to decision making.

In this interview begin to practice using prompts to move the interview forward and probes to move the interview deeper. Maintain and sharpen the skills and abilities you have already learned.

After you have completed tape-recording your interview, listen to it with a pad and pen handy, noting each time you used one of your new counseling skills and abilities. You should be pleasantly surprised and reinforced to see how far you have come as a counselor during this short but concentrated training program.

In addition to the "Taped Interview Analysis," you may wish to make a Give-and-Take Interview Review Chart for keeping track of the progress of your interview while listening to it, similar to the one below.

---

**Chart 5.1 GIVE-AND-TAKE INTERVIEW REVIEW (Sample)**

Client Statement 1 (key words/themes only) _____

_____

Counselor Response 1 (stated in full) _____

_____

Type of Counseling Skill Used _____

_____

Client Statement 2 (key words/themes only) _____

_____

Counselor Response 2 (stated in full) _____

_____

Type of Counseling Skill Used _____

_____

Etc. _____

_____

_____

_____

---

Chapter Five **BACK TALK**

Please answer the following questions for this chapter:

1. What is the main point of this chapter? _____

_____

_____

_____

_____

2. What was your favorite illustration/story in this chapter? Why? _____

_____

_____

_____

_____

3. Describe a personal experience you have had as a counselor or counselee
(formal or informal) that relates to the content of this chapter: _____

_____

_____

_____

_____

4. What question(s) do you have after reading this chapter? _____

_____

_____

_____

_____

5. What would you like to learn more about in this course? _____

_____

_____

_____

_____

Chapter Five  **TAPED INTERVIEW ANALYSIS**

Name: _____

Date: _____

Interview Number: _____

1. What was the client's presenting (initial) problem or opportunity?_____

_____

_____

_____

2. What skills did you attempt to practice in this interview? Give one or more

examples: _____

_____

_____

_____

3. What do you feel you did best in this interview? _____

_____

_____

_____

4. What do you feel you need to improve upon based on this interview? ____

_____

_____

_____

5. Describe any surprises, shifts in direction or content, or significant positive

or negative turning points in this interview: _____

_____

_____

_____

6. How was the client thinking and/or feeling by the end of this interview? __

_____

_____

_____

_____

7. If this were an interview series, what do you think might happen in the next interview?_____

_____

_____

_____

_____

8. What did you learn most about the process of personal counseling from conducting this interview? _____

_____

_____

_____

_____

Chapter Five **THE COUNSELOR'S LIBRARY**

Consider adding one or more of these books to your counseling library:

Augsburger, David. *Caring Enough to Confront.* Glendale, Cal.: GL/Regal Books, 1974.
> This small paperback was originally designed to teach couples to confront each other within the marriage relationship. It will also be helpful to the pastoral counselor who needs to grow in this area.

Egan, Gerard. *Exercises in Helping Skills.* Fifth edition. Belmont, Cal.: Brooks/ Cole Publishing Company, 1994.
> One of the finest counseling practice workbooks ever published, this manual is coordinated with *The Skilled Helper* textbook by the same author but is highly effective in its own right. The effective use of prompts and probes is a major feature.

Hemfelt, Robert, and Richard Fowler, Eds. *Serenity: A Companion for 12 Step Recovery.* Nashville: Thomas Nelson, 1990.
> This New Testament with Psalms and Proverbs has key Twelve-Step commentary and Scripture indexing throughout. You will find it invaluable in working with persons who are trying to recover from drug and alcohol addictions. It is also very helpful for other people with a wide range of life's problems.

Miller, J. Keith. *A Hunger for Healing.* San Franciso: Harper, 1991.
> Keith Miller may be America's most outstanding Christian communicator on the subject of recovery. This book shows how the classic Twelve Steps can serve as an exciting model for Christian growth and spiritual maturity. An excellent video series by the same name is also available.

Doc & Duck © 1999 Andrew J. Cheydleur

# Advanced Action-Planning Skills

*A young woman with a BSW degree from Rutgers University joined our Salvation Army staff, "because I want to work for a Christian agency." During several months of getting to know her, we discovered she was attempting to get her spiritual guidance through smoking pot rather than through prayer, even though she professed to being a Christian.*

*As a consequence her moral perceptions were distorted, as was her general ability to do long-range planning and reality testing in important life issues such as finances and personal relationships.*

*Through spiritual coaching and action planning with other staff members, she eventually chose to join a very wonderful Spirit-filled church, completely gave up smoking marijuana, and began to find wisdom from God in prayer, which proved to be more satisfying than her drug-enhanced introspective illusions.*

IN THE ACTION-PLANNING process, the "counselor" role changes to that of a "coach," encouraging clients to help themselves through creative planning, spiritual accountability, and aftercare.

The ideal end product and goal of faith-based counseling and case management is for clients to become Spirit led and Bible directed. This enables them to be self-sustaining with God rather than dependant upon the counselor as the primary resource for problem analysis, resolution, and action planning.

As Dr. Gerard Egan states in his very practical book *The Skilled Helper,* "Listening for the sake of listening, exploring for the sake of exploring, and challenging for the sake of challenging are all useless. The work to this point is successful if it leads to the kind of problem clarification that contributes to the establishment of realistic, problem-handling goals." Certainly a great deal of psychological research would support Dr. Egan in his perception that "helping clients set goals cannot be over stressed."

From a scriptural perspective, the ultimate goal is to bring clients to the point where they can receive wisdom directly from God. To do this, they need sufficient discernment to know which voices are of the Lord and which voices are from evil spirits or narcissistic imagination. "If any of you lacks wisdom, let him ask of God, who gives to all men liberally and without reproach, and it will be given to him. But let him ask in faith, with no doubting, for he who doubts is like a wave of the sea driven and tossed by the wind. For let not that man suppose that he will receive anything from the Lord; he is a double-minded man, unstable in all his ways" (James 1:5-8). A solid grounding in the book of Proverbs can moderate a great deal of foolish thinking.

## Going beyond Introspection

Leanne Payne, one of the foremost Christian teachers of prayer in relation to mental health, tells the story of a young man in counseling who described his situation to her.

> *"I stand back and look at myself and logically go over everything I can't stand about myself—my walk, the way I look, my mannerisms, etc."*
>
> *The young man constantly did this. Just as a scientist studies a bug or a flower by dissecting it, so this young man regularly pinned himself to his own dissecting table, fragmenting himself in the process.*
>
> *His healing would never come until he stopped this pernicious activity (of extreme introspection). I told him in no uncertain terms what he was doing and led him to repent and turn from that diseased emotional view of the self.*
>
> *Then I taught him the kind of prayer that enabled him to take deep droughts of the Spirit of God (the ultimate in Objective Real outside himself) back into him. His difficulty was, he had never accepted himself, and his self-criticism and even self-hatred manifested itself in this way.*
>
> *The cure? Teaching him to look up and out. "But as a Christian I have to examine myself, don't I?" he asked in some amazement. He was right, but as I always say to these sufferers, in looking up to God—that is, asking Him to come in and shine His light into my heart—I get involved with real things, what's really there. And I receive an objective good, either forgiveness or illumination. I am not indulging in diseased attitudes toward the self.*
>
> The Healing Presence, *pages 158–159*

In a very real sense, the task of counseling is to help clients work through their narcissistic double-mindedness and doubt so that they can clearly receive wisdom from the Lord.

In moving toward the conclusion of a series of counseling interviews, a counselor becomes acutely aware of the client's need to build a reality-based platform for personal growth in the future. For the counselor, this very likely will include:

- a summary of the gains made in counseling this far;
- some review of the insights that the client has demonstrated; and
- an affirmation of the value commitments the client has worked through and personally endorsed.

This process should already have resulted in a movement from the neurotic introspection that brought the client to counseling in the first place to a more objective emphasis on prayer and other external realities.

In order to keep the client from returning to a diseased introspection, it is most often helpful to have some clearly defined action plans for the future. This is complemented by an agreed-upon accountability to an individual or a group to support the commitment for completing the action plans. Both the action plans and the plans for accountability should be specific and include timetables, specific persons, models, places, organizations, programs, inner experiences, and outer resources.

Of course, you will always want to "keep the door open" for emergency follow-up contacts, and you may actually want to plan some specific follow-ups, perhaps at three- or six-month intervals.

Fabricant and Linn suggest that one of the most effective forms of long-term action planning is to teach clients various ways to pray, which they can utilize in the absence of a counselor. In their *Prayer Workbook on Healing Life's Hurts* (pages 20-22), they teach a variety of approaches to prayer, including such ideas as "A body gratitude prayer," "A hand prayer," "A sleep prayer," "A walk-of-thanksgiving prayer," "Awareness prayer," etc. One of their prayer suggestions is based on re-creating an experience of love

and beauty. The gratitude such a prayer may evoke can be an excellent antidote for negative introspection.

> *Recall a moment when you felt deeply loved. Recall the beauty you felt within*
> *yourself and the sense of your own goodness. Reexperience that moment, thank-*
> *ing God for revealing to you the wonderful person He sees when He looks*
> *at you.*

The more prayer models a person has to choose from in order to approach
God under various circumstances, the more he or she is able to be self-
sustaining in his or her spiritual life and to receive guidance and affirmation
from God rather than having those needs met by a counselor.

## Creating Clear and Specific Goals

> *As I have shared earlier, while doing my first counseling internship at*
> *Lakeview-Uptown Mental Health Clinic in Chicago, the clinic psychiatrist*
> *assigned me a young homosexual man who had asked for a "young, white, male*
> *therapist." Coming out of my background of serving as a Salvation Army corps*
> *officer, my primary interest was in evangelizing him to become a Christian; his*
> *interest was in seducing me into the gay lifestyle. Larry's history included*
> *having been seduced by his first psychiatrist at age fourteen and, more recently,*
> *of having seduced a number of young male counselors in an attempt to reassert*
> *some power over his own life. Larry was also abusing prescription drugs and*
> *was failing financially. Our first five or six interviews consisted primarily of*
> *dancing around the two issues we both brought to the table. I tried to get him to*
> *go to church, and he tried to get me to visit the local gay bar scene in order to*
> *"understand the gay culture."*
>
> *Once I began to understand that Larry was not about to become converted*
> *to Christianity, and he understood I was not about to become converted to the*
> *gay lifestyle, we were able to attain a measure of respect for each other as indi-*
> *viduals and move to the point where creating clear and specific goals was*
> *appropriate. However, Larry had been in treatment at some very prestigious*
> *hospital-based psychiatric facilities, where he had been videotaped, had been*
> *interviewed by a variety of psychiatric residents, and had achieved a kind*
> *of celebrity status. It was, of course, much easier for him to talk about these*
> *experiences, as well as his experiences of having seduced young male counselors,*
> *being involved in "cruising" activities, and feeling the rush of the dramatic in*
> *the various activities associated with his lifestyle. It was harder for him to talk*
> *about his abuse of prescription drugs, but even here he enjoyed talking about his*
> *extensive knowledge of the PDR and the fact that he had "quart bottles of*
> *Haldol" and other drugs on the window ledge of his room.*

*While the use of empathy skills was important in building a relationship with this bright young man, Larry's ultimate needs were for practical, commonplace living, and a sense of autonomy and independence from his parents. Therefore, the work of counseling became that of helping his practical goals to become clear and helping him to look at the methods and activities he would have to undertake to achieve those goals.*

*I helped Larry commit to the mundane tasks of planning a job-search routine, define the type of living quarters he desired, and look at what kind of practical, ordinary disciplines he would need to commit to in order to hold a job that would maintain the kind of economic independence he desired. As he developed these goals, I was able to support him in them, and together we worked through an action plan for professional employment, which he successfully implemented and became a customer-service person for a major airline.*

One of the ways you can tell when a counseling series is "wrapping itself up" is when the client is able to create clear and specific goals and begins to act on them.

---

**Skill Builder 6.1**  In the exercises below, first write an empathy response to the client's statement; then write some possible goals and activities you could imagine yourself exploring with this client at a later stage of the counseling process.

A. *Client:* "I just don't really see myself going anywhere anymore. I dropped out of high school in eleventh grade, and while I do have a trade, it doesn't pay very well, and my wife is on my back all the time because we don't have enough money to do the things she wants to do for the kids, and I feel like I am sort of a used-up, unhappy person without much hope."

*Empathy Response:* _____

_____

_____

*Long-term Goals:* _____

_____

_____

*Immediate Activities:* _____

_____

_____

B. *Client:* "I can't believe I am fifty-eight years old and am still having problems in all my relationships with men! This includes my boss, my husband, and our two grown sons as well as others. I think it might have something to do with the fact that my uncle raped me when I was eleven years old, but everybody I try to talk with about this says that at my age I ought to simply grow up and forget about it. It shouldn't affect how I relate to other men, since they didn't do it."

Empathy Response: _____

_____

_____

Long-Term Goals: _____

_____

_____

Immediate Activities: _____

_____

_____

## Using Baseline Data to Break Through Denial

*In a series of premarital counseling sessions, a young couple planned to go through the seven routine checkpoints that I normally use in this type of counseling. They were compatible about values, money, sexual attitudes, etc. On what was supposed to be the last interview, I realized that somehow we had never talked about children. We had simply managed to talk about all the other issues and never discussed this one. Before they went out the door, I raised the issue about how they felt about children. The man said, "Oh, I've had a vasectomy, so we won't have any children; therefore, it is not an issue!" The wife-to-be, a young woman in her early thirties, looked absolutely flabbergasted! I realized I had not asked them each to get a physical and share the results.*

Sometimes, of course, it is the trivial that is first presented and the important that is being denied. In order for the counselor not to be seduced by the client's manipulations, it is important to have a structured interview process. You can comprehensively look at those things that are going well and those that are going poorly in the client's life. Some residential Christian agencies, such as The Salvation Army's Adult Rehabilitation Centers, use a structured psychosocial interview form to insure that adequate baseline data is collected at intake.

In a totally unstructured interview process, it is possible to overlook key reality issues, since an intelligent, manipulative client can find many things to talk about other than those which are the major problems!

The most serious and critical issues of life are often the ones that are talked around, avoided, and never raised. Therefore, the final development of

adequate action plans depends on the counselor's keeping a mental or written checklist of the critical issues discussed earlier. The counselor helps the client look at all data in order to acknowledge the problems that need to be discussed and dealt with.

**Skill Builder 6.2** In the following exercises, first write an empathy or empathy-sandwich response; then imagine some missing data that could be the cause of or solution to what is being discussed, which the client has not yet clearly stated.

A. *Client:* "I am really just here to get some groceries today. You know, it's the middle of the month, and it's hard to stretch the welfare check. My husband couldn't come with me, because the only chance he has to take a nap is when I take the kids out of the house."

*Empathy Response:* _____

_____

_____

_____

*Possible Hidden Data:* _____

_____

_____

_____

**B.** *Client:* "I'm real sorry, Miss Sally, about not showing up for band practice last night, but I kind of hurt my wrist when I fell off my bicycle, and besides that, I am not sure I am really good enough to play or to be in the junior band, or maybe I should be a vocalist."

*Empathy Response:* _____

_____

_____

*Possible Hidden Data:* _____

_____

_____

## Inviting Creative Alternatives

*When I was serving as Dr. Egan's graduate assistant at Loyola University in Chicago, he took a number of us counselors-in-training to Wisconsin one weekend to do group therapy and conduct communications-training sessions with an order of nuns. This had previously been a silent order, and the nuns were now learning to communicate with each other in words and spoken emotions. It was really quite a marvelous experience, filled with laughter, tears, excitement, and the struggle of these devout women to relearn how to use verbal communication in a way that they had been prevented from doing for many years.*

*Part of the training process of that weekend was designed to help these women become specific and clear in their communications with each other, not allowing themselves to cloak difficult communications in vague or pious generalities.*

Clients who have grown up in restrictive or abusive environments may hesitate to suggest any of their own solutions. They may wait until they receive a clue to what the counselor's position is on the topic. One creative counselor reduces clients' fears of coming up with their own ideas by using such statements as, "Let's think up three or four different ways we could approach this problem. It doesn't matter how off-the-wall they are, just that you get a chance to practice your imagination and thinking skills at this time. We can come back and evaluate these later." This part of the counseling process, so different from the early-stage issues of empathy, positive regard, and value sorting, is critical to helping the client become skilled in practices that will be self-sustaining.

Help clients make it a habit to always think of more than one possible approach to a problem. This releases them from internal self-criticism, which results if a particular approach fails or cannot be implemented. Since the client is personally creating alternatives, all of them bring equal satisfaction. None of them is an only choice, as all have been borne out of the client's own creativity, prayer, and planning.

In the brainstorming process, such creativity-killing questions as "What if it doesn't work?" should be routinely replaced by such creativity-expanding questions as "What if it *does* work?" This type of positive prompt extends the range of possibilities, options, and preparations for coping with success. Many small successes are needed to replace previous experiences of restricted options, wrong choices, and being forced to cope with failure.

As the client becomes increasingly clear about needs and opportunities, and we have helped him or her move out of shallow introspection into a deep arena of prayer and spiritual guidance, we also need to move away

from our "parental" role toward the client. We allow God the Father His role in becoming the continuing counselor for this individual. As the great theologian G. Campbell Morgan states:

*The indwelling Spirit knows the Will of God and interprets it to the soul in whom He abides. This He does by unveiling Christ, who is the revelation of the Will of God to me. As He was the Word of God incarnate, He was the Will of God incarnate. I come to Him that I may see what is God's Will for myself and for all men; that I may understand what is God's purpose concerning the whole world. . . .*

*As the Spirit interprets to us the Will of God, He shows the disaster of being out of harmony with that Will. As the Spirit interprets the Will of God, therefore, He makes the soul profoundly discontented with everything that is contrary thereto, and this because of the soul's supreme content with the good and perfect and acceptable Will of God.*

The Practice of Prayer, *pages 58-59*

In other words, we need to rejoice as the client's own intuitive and perceptive faculties increasingly come into play, demonstrating that the client has the opportunity to hear the voice and direction of God just as much as does the counselor!

**Skill Builder 6.3** In the following exercises, write a "brainstorming invitation" that invites the client to look at alternative approaches and action plans.

A. *Client:* "Well, with everything messed up at home and all, and money being the way it is, I just don't see any choice except to join the stupid Marines!"

*Brainstorming Invitation:* _____

_____

_____

B. *Client:* "I mean, I didn't even do anything really wrong. But somehow it's me who gets noticed. Like, the only choice I see now is to either drop out of the dumb school or stay there and get a bad rap!"

*Brainstorming Invitation:* _____

_____

_____

## Pruning and Organizing Ideas

> *Lynn was a secretary, single and thirty-six years old. Her biological clock was ticking. She had met many men, but they were not "fun."*
>
> *After listing many characteristics she might want in a future husband, she zeroed in on "somebody who likes to square-dance." So she started a singles' square-dance club at the local Y. There she met her husband-to-be.*

Your client has been through the brainstorming process and has created a wide number of options and possibilities. This must be followed up with a process of pruning and organizing all of these ideas to end up with a functional set of behavioral goals and programs to accomplish those goals. Typically, the steps in this process include the following:

a. *Declaration of wishes or intent.* At this stage a client might be wishing something like: "I would like to be happier at work."
b. *More specific focus of hope.* In the example above, the counselee might prune his or her general concern for being happier at work to a more concrete hope, such as: "I would like to have my boss tell me something good about my work at least two or three times a month instead of always being on my case."
c. *Specific behavioral faith goals.* Now, with the help of the counselor, the client might move away from concern about what the boss does and move toward

the specific behavioral goals that he or she has faith to achieve: "I would like to specifically plan two pieces of work each month that I know match the boss's priorities and get credit for doing those pieces of work well."

d. *Program commitment to accomplish the goals.* Then, moving from the client's goal to the program to accomplish it, the client might make the commitment: "In order to do that, I will have to stop eating lunch at my desk. I will eat lunch in the cafeteria with the boss and the other three people that he kicks ideas around with, so I can understand what his priorities are, since he never communicates them in the office but only around the lunch table."

---

**Skill Builder 6.4** In the following exercises, use your imagination to complete sections B, C, and D as though the client were working through the goal-setting process with you.

A. *Client's Declaration of Wishes or Intent:* "Well, I am seventeen years old, and I would really like to do something to help in this messed-up world. Staying in school seems to be pretty dull, but I don't exactly know whether I want to be a pastor, a social worker, join the Peace Corps, or just exactly what. I would like to feel I have a sense of meaning and significance helping other people."

B. *Client's Specific Focus of Hope:* _____

_____

_____

C. *Client's Specific Behavioral Faith Goals:* _____

_____

_____

D. *Client's Program Commitment to Accomplish the Goals:* _____

_____

_____

---

## Moving from Counselor to Coach

*During an extremely difficult period of personal career transition, I used to go for coaching several times a week to meet with an older Greek friend in San Diego. Nick is a short, compact, practical Christian man who spent several years of his childhood in Greece hiding (with his mother) from invading Italian soldiers; later he was a used-car salesman and pastor in the USA before becoming the successful and wealthy owner of a small chain of nursing homes.*

*Nick would invite me into his kitchen and pour out two thimble-sized cups of thick Greek coffee, and talk with me about my future, keeping my feet on the ground when I wanted to spin fanciful possibilities. Nick is the most direct, "shoot-from-the-hip" person I have ever known.*

*He taught me to use "Nick's Nine," a terrific set of practical questions, which he used over and over again with me until I learned to use them without additional coaching.*

In this latter stage of counseling and planning, you are actually moving from the empathetic role of listener and supporter to a more structured role as trainer and organizer, so this does take some change in counselor perspective as well as in client perspective. In the role of trainer and organizer, the counselor helps the client learn the processes that make personal goals clear and specific. The counselor uses prayer and Scripture as well as laughter and self-analysis to establish workable, God-honoring, sustainable goals. As the client learns this

process through the counseling experience, he or she also becomes able to replicate the process outside of the counseling experience.

The following questions will help your client turn positive fantasies into practical realities:

NICK'S NINE
1. What is the goal you really want to achieve?
2. Whom do you know who can help you make this goal work?
3. What resources or strengths do these people have?
4. Do you have any resources yourself that you can use to achieve this goal?
5. Where do you need to go to make your goal become reality?
6. When are you going to work on this goal (timing)?
7. What forces or people are holding you back from achieving this goal?
8. What can you do to block, remove, or avoid any opposing forces?
9. If your goal can't be achieved all at once, what part of it are you willing to tackle first?

During this process it is important that the client not be allowed to become introspective or self-critical but that he or she be encouraged simply to produce a large quantity of ideas. The process of analyzing, sorting, and linking those ideas is a secondary process.

**Skill Builder 6.5** Using the "Nick's Nine" formula listed in this chapter, evaluate the following plan.

## CLIENT'S STATEMENT

*Client:* "I think if I join the army, Pamela will quit liking Bill and start liking me, because all girls are suckers for a man in uniform. Besides, its time I moved out of my folks' house and became a man on my own, and my uncle Ernie is an Army Recruiting Sergeant in the next town over. I just hope my mom and my dog Joe won't miss me too much when I'm gone to boot camp."

## EVALUATION

Real Goal:_____

_____

People You Know/Their Resources:_____

_____

Your Resources: _____

_____

Where to Go: _____

_____

When: _____

_____

What's Holding You Back:_____

_____

How to Remove Any Blocks: _____

_____

What Happens First: _____

_____

## Choosing Action-Program Elements

*When my son Jim graduated from Columbia University, he wanted to move back to California and try to break into the music business. He asked me what kind of car he should buy. Should he buy a used sports car or a used VW mini-bus? In terms of control, he had just enough money to afford either. In terms of relevance, he decided the sports car could attract girls while the van could carry a drum set, guitars, and musicians. The van won out because the music goal was more attractive to him. Eventually, his band signed with SONY, made a CD, and went on tour.*

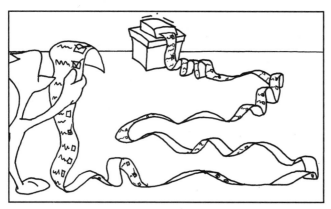

After most of the ideas are produced and written down, the coach helps the client organize them and choose specific program elements. To help in this process of choosing, Dr. Egan teaches a planning-review formula, entitled C-R-A-V-E. The five elements of this formula are used to evaluate the proposed action plan, which was developed through the brainstorming process. Ask these five questions to help your client evaluate the plan that you and your client have developed together.

> **C—Control** To what degree does your client have control over the proposed course of action, including access to the resources needed to engage in it?
>
> **R—Relevancy** Will this possible course of action actually lead to getting the goal accomplished, or is it only partly related to the goal, even if it turns out to be successful?
>
> **A—Attractiveness** Does this possible course of action really appeal to the client, or is it something he or she is passively agreeing to just to please the counselor or someone else?
>
> **V—Values** Is this possible course of action in keeping with the client's values and moral standards?
>
> **E—Environment** Is this possible course of action free from major obstacles in the physical or social environment?

In sorting out the various possibilities that have been generated through brainstorming, the client could actually make a chart. He or she can list all the ideas and then rate them on each of the five C-R-A-V-E elements. In practicing this with the counselor, the client is also being trained for a process that he or she can then use in the future for other problems and situations.

**Skill Builder 6.6**  Make a C-R-A-V-E chart to evaluate the following plan.

*Client:* "I'm almost finished here at the drug rehab, and I called my mother, who says I can stay with her if my uncle Henry will give me a job at the box factory. If I can get him to let me work the night shift, then I could probably go to the community college during the day. I could still go to some evening Narcotics Anonymous meeting, to help keep me sober. What do you think?"

C—Control (Who controls this decision/these resources?): _____

_____

R—Relevancy (Can this action plan actually lead to the desired goal?): \_\_\_\_\_

_____

A—Attractiveness (Is this a plan that "looks good" to the client?): _____

_____

V—Values (Is this plan in keeping with the client's highest values?): _____

_____

E—Environment (Will other people and events support this plan?): _____

_____

## Coaching for Goals

*One day I was walking across the parking lot between classes with one of my graduate students, and was he angry! He would have kicked rocks if there had been any loose ones in that parking lot! Trying to get at what was bothering him, I humorously remarked, "Your problem, Sam, is that you don't want to be a student, you want to be on the faculty!" His anger was punctuated with a loud burst of laughter. This led to our being able to think about some concrete goals and action plans for him to regain some of his self-esteem. He realized he had temporarily surrendered his professional status by moving to graduate school and out of a career in direct social work. He began to facilitate some counseling groups for other students, later ran for student elective office, and after graduation was hired as a supervisor in a large mental-health agency, where he was allowed to take on teaching responsibilities.*

For some of your clients, the process of planning goals is difficult in itself. The long history of broken New Year's resolutions tells us that for most, the problem with goals is usually not in the initial task of creating some sort of goal statement. Instead, the problem lies in the longer-term question of following through on goals that are important to the person's future.

As a counselor/coach, you help the client to sort those goals that are important enough to become commitments from those goals that are perhaps attractive, but not actually powerful enough for follow-through.

Help the client to develop appropriately structured goal timetables.

Can a profitable new business be developed in one month's time? Most likely not, given that most new businesses experience a negative cash flow for the first one or two years! These are three tests that need to be looked at in the developing of goal timetables:

1. *Is the timetable reasonable?* That is, does it compare with the normal amount of time that other people have experienced in achieving similar goals?
2. *Is the timetable specific?* That is, are we just talking about doing this some time, or "after I get old," or some other vague term? Or have we laid this out in a specific way, so the client will know that he or she has either accomplished the goal or failed to accomplish the goal by a certain date or some kind of equally definable benchmark?
3. *Are interim steps included?* It is all very well to say I will build a vacation house prior to my retirement or rebuild a close relationship with my estranged daughter, but what are the steps that must be taken toward these goals? And what is the specific timetable and sequence for these steps to be completed on the way to the goal? Until the interim steps are laid out and a timetable for them is prayed through, even if in some

flexible fashion, the goals remain "magical," because without the interim steps, the jump to goal completion would indeed take magic!

**Skill Builder 6.7** Imagine the following situation, and write a brief timetable for accomplishing the indicated goal.

A. *Client:* "Pastor, I feel like I am being called into the ministry just like you, and I have picked out a Bible College I want to go to. However, my wife and I both need to save some money before I can go. We have to think about what is right for the children as well. Also, we have to find a way to get out of the lease on our house. We also need to think about whether we can afford to keep either of the cars we have. Could you help me?"

B. Brief Sample Timetable:

1. _____

_____

_____

2. _____

_____

_____

3. _____

_____

_____

4. _____

_____

_____

C. Review the above timetable, which you have created, on the basis of the following questions:

1. Is the timetable reasonable? _____

_____

_____

2. Is the timetable specific? _____

_____

_____

3. Are interim steps included?_____

_____

_____

## Facing the Future Spiritually

> *There is not in the world a kind of life more sweet and delightful than that of a continual conversation with God. Those only can comprehend it who practice and experience it; yet I do not advise you to do it from that motive. It is not pleasure which we ought to seek in this exercise; but let us do it from a principle of love, and because God would have us. . . .*
>
> *Ah! Do we but want . . . the grace and assistance of God, we should never lose sight of Him—no, not for a moment. . . . I cannot imagine how religious persons can live satisfied without the practice of the presence of God."*
>
> *Brother Lawrence*

Help the client analyze personal resources and environmental challenges: intelligence, money, determination, spirituality, resource groups, support, opposing persons, and postive and negative social and spiritual forces related to the selected goals.

The focus of this process is to be clear and honest about what things are controllable and what things are not controllable, which are related to the person's goals. Many otherwise fine goals are derailed by a person's pretending to him- or herself that forces or people that he or she has no control over will somehow cooperate with him or her. On the other hand, many notable goals are never established because a person is afraid of people or forces over which some control could be exercised.

Often the necessary perspective for sane, spiritual thinking that is neither overly positive nor overly negative must first come in the quiet contemplation and meditation of prayer. Nicholas Herman, the French soldier who became a Carmelite monk in the year 1666 and was later known as "Brother Lawrence," achieved serenity, peace, and perspective through prayer, although his assigned job at the monastery was the lowly one of dishwasher. In between doing the dishes, he wrote in his now famous journal, *The Practice of the Presence of God.*

From a Christian perspective, the development of a sane, sensitive spirituality is a critical goal of the counseling process. It is vitally important to a person's being able to plan and to correctly and evenly evaluate the risk and potential involved in the planning process.

---

**Skill Builder 6.8** Fabricant and Linn suggest a six-step prayer technique for facing the future. Clients are fearful about the decisions they have to make and the outcome of those decisions (*Prayer Workbook for Healing Life's Hurts*, page 151). Practice this technique on yourself before trying it with someone you are counseling:

1. Read Luke 22:39-42—The agony in the Garden.

2. Ask Jesus to help you create in your imagination the scene of what you most fear or want to be able to face in the future.

3. Face the fear or hurt (or possibility of success) until you feel it in your body. Share how you feel with Jesus.

4. Ask Jesus to help you absorb how He would respond to the same situation—His thoughts and feelings.
   A. What does Jesus want done to prevent what He fears ("Remove this . . .")?
   B. How does Jesus promise that growth will come if it is the Father's will for you to go through what you most fear to face?
      1. How would Jesus go through it?
      2. What would He say, do, see, etc.?
      3. In your imagination, react like Jesus.
   C. After doing this, what is still difficult for you to face?
      1. How does Jesus find a gift in this fear?

5. Live out Jesus' reaction by taking one step to face this fear (e.g., take a step closer to the feared cliff; if you fear death, make out a will, etc.).

6. Thank Jesus for whatever has happened during the prayer and rest in His strength.

---

## Coaching for Independence

*One of my counseling mentors, the late Dr. (Father) Charles Curran, who was president of the American Catholic Psychological Association, took me aside one time and told me how to tell a good pastoral counselor from a mediocre one. "Look at the wall behind his desk," Dr. Curran declared with a characteristic chuckle and a twinkle in his eye, "and see how many Christmas cards and notes he has posted there. If there are too many, it means he has failed as a counselor because his people are still depending on him rather than on God or on themselves!"*

Aftercare may include continuing contact with the counselor and a reduced counseling frequency or a more widely spaced interval between sessions. It may also include an agreed-upon method for contacting the counselor in emergencies or for reestablishing the counseling relationship if/when new problems arise. However, the ideal aftercare/accountability plan will also include the following activities not related to the counselor:

**A regular plan of prayer and Bible study** This allows the client to sort out problems, receive spiritual guidance, and reinforce Christian values alone with God and/or in the context of a weekly small-group fellowship.

**An agreed-upon plan of accountability/support** This can be done with one or more mentoring individuals or a small group who will help monitor specific progress in regard to the client's selected goals and activity programs. This plan should include specific people who have agreed to help in this way and, at the beginning of the plan, should also specify specific intervals for contact with these people. An accountability support group is critical for anyone struggling with an addiction.

**Specific source(s) for any planned training, education, or technical/ social/spiritual support** This should be identified and membership fees paid or other commitments initiated prior to the end of the counseling process.

**Necessary materials for any "inner work" such as assigned reading, writing, or keeping a journal** These should be secured and this activity should begin during the counseling process, so any necessary alterations or corrections to it may be negotiated while the counselor is still available.

**A clear appointment now for a six-months-later "checkup interview"** This is often a valuable accountability tool in helping the client continue and maintain his or her aftercare program.

## After Counseling Is Completed

You can teach your client a personal program-review system to use to look at programs that he or she designs to meet future goals. There are six questions that you can teach a client to ask. These will be particularly helpful when the client is no longer in counseling.

1. **Is this program realistic for me?** Here we are asking the client to evaluate whether he or she has done something like this before that has succeeded. He or she looks at whether the amount of time and finances required are available. He or she asks whether his or her own fear or expectation level might sabotage the process. He or she checks to see whether his or

her sense of moral and spiritual responsibility will work for or against the envisioned activity. David made this type of self-evaluation in 1 Samuel 17:36, when he stated, "Your servant has killed both lion and bear; and this uncircumcised Philistine will be like one of them."

**2. Is this activity program adequate for my intended purpose?** This may be the question that is most overlooked by people designing personal programs to meet goals. Charlie's program (for instance, of taking dance lessons) may have value in itself. It may not meet his larger goal of winning approval and support from his wife, Helen, to move the family to another city. Even though an activity program may have been suggested by other significant people, it may not be adequate to actually obtain the intended result. Often clients attempt "desperate measures" in order to win someone's love. They try to fulfill a dream without recognizing that even if the activity program is successful, the larger goal may not be fulfilled.

**3. Does this program match my deeply held spiritual values?** No program or activity our clients engage in will be beneficial in the long term if it runs against deeply held spiritual values. The coach's training task is to teach the client to ask him- or herself this question. It does not always have to be prompted by the counselor or other people. A well-developed prayer relationship with God is obviously helpful to this process. You help the client develop a stable prayer pattern by working with him or her to help clarify his or her deeply held spiritual values during the counseling process. This allows him or her to have a clear and reliable spiritual benchmark against which to compare program ideas.

**4. Are the likely consequences of achieving this goal acceptable to me?** All over America, to take an outrageous example, there are people whose goal is to win one million dollars in the lottery. Their activity program is to buy a one-dollar lottery ticket each week until they win! Even if we were naive enough to believe that this program of activity could actually attain that particular goal, there would still be the question of whether or not these individuals are prepared for the negative consequences of being instant millionaires!

Are they ready to pay taxes to the IRS? Are they ready to have investment counselors knocking at their door and calling them up at all hours of the day and night? Are they willing to have every shirttail relative who was never nice to them before decide to drop by and tell them they are the greatest people on earth? Are they willing to have to screen all new relationships to determine whether the motive is really personal or whether it is financial? Of course, there could also be many benefits to being an instant millionaire, but there are certainly some negative issues as well. When a person establishes a goal and then establishes a program to meet that goal, he or she needs to look at whether or not the consequences, both positive and negative, will be acceptable to him or her if the goal is in fact reached!

5. **Can I sustain this activity program for a long enough period of time for the goal to be achieved?** Although, in the above ridiculous example, the activity program might never succeed in reaching the goal of winning the lottery, it is in fact sustainable. Most people can put a dollar a week into any purpose, however frivolous, without being materially affected in a negative way. However, suppose one of these people had formulated his or her goal as wanting to win one million dollars in the lottery? What if that person had then defined his or her activity program as putting his or her entire paycheck into the lottery every week to increase the chances of winning more quickly? This activity program, although it would increase the chances of success somewhat, would not be sustainable. If the person did not win soon, he or she would begin to have problems with car payments, mortgage payments, food, and other financial obligations in short order. The sustainability of a program, especially if it may take a longer time to succeed than initially predicted, is a critical part of the program-review process.

6. **Does this program of activity include room for God's activity (leading to gratitude), or does it only leave room for personal achievement (leading to pride)?** In a sense, this question suggests a false polarity. The use of one's personal abilities is not necessarily opposed to God's doing things in one's life. However, the question needs to be raised because a person who develops an inflated sense of self may later sabotage the very success he or she has created. All of us need to learn that God "fills the hungry soul with goodness" (Ps. 107:9) and that genuine supernatural forces do come into play. God does help the person who is humbly conscious of his/her own limitations. Such a person desires more than just goal accomplishment. He or she also wants a sense of closeness with God: "Blessed are those who hunger and thirst for righteousness, for they shall be filled" (Matt. 5:6).

**Skill Builder 6.9** Practice action planning at a personal level by briefly describing some type of personal activity program you are contemplating doing during the next year. This could be related to personal devotions, such as Bible study or prayer. Or this activity program could relate to personal fitness, such as weight loss or muscle training. This program could relate to intellectual attainment, such as reading or writing in the area of a certain topic. Any worthwhile activity/goal is acceptable for this training exercise.

Describe your proposed goal and the activity needed to implement it: _____

_____

_____

_____

_____

Now answer the following C-R-A-V-E questions

**C**ONTROL - Is this program realistic for me? _____

_____

_____

**R**ELEVANCY - Is this activity program appropriate for my intended purpose? _

_____

_____

**A**TTRACTIVENESS - Do I really like this idea? _____

_____

_____

**V**ALUES - How is this activity program congruent with my most deeply held spiritual values? _____

_____

_____

**E**NVIRONMENT - Are there people and resources available to support me in this program? _____

_____

_____

1. Are the possible consequences of this program (positive or negative) acceptable? _____

_____

_____

_____

2. Can I sustain this activity program for a long enough period of time for it to work? _____

_____

_____

_____

## Practicing Your Role As "Coach"

The listening, challenging, value-sorting, prayer, and Scripture input of faith-based counseling are all designed to assist the client in moving out of a self-defeating cycle of introspection, doubt, and ineffective activity based on conflicting and/or little-understood values.

During this process the client reexamines personal values and former decisions in the light of Scripture, prayer, and common sense. This prepares the client for the exciting but difficult work of creating new goals that are clear, specific, and attainable.

Also, during this process your role changes subtly from listener and spiritual supporter to coach and practical organizer.

Now you and your client practice working together to review and strengthen goals and their supporting activities for the future, so they will be realistic, adequate, spiritual, acceptable, and sustainable.

Following the completion of the counseling/coaching experience, the client will continue to reinforce his/her progress with regular prayer and Bible study, an accountability support group, appropriate training and education, personal-growth homework, and a planned "checkup" interview with you.

The Skill Builders should prove helpful to you in preparing for this final and most important part of the counseling process.

After completing the Skill Builders, you are ready to conduct and record your practice counseling interview in this series. As you have done during the prior interviews, ask a friend, another student, or a family member to work with you on this exercise. It is particularly important for this exercise that he or she talk about something real, not anything imaginary, and not any type of role play.

For the purposes of this taped interview, you may wish to select a person with whom you have already been counseling. As an alternative, select someone you know who has some type of goal in mind that he or she has spent some time thinking about, so that planning is now the appropriate stage of the counseling/coaching process for that person.

Plan this interview for approximately one hour in length, and have your client bring pen/pencil and paper to the interview, so the two of you can work together to practice some of the planning exercises.

During the review of your counseling tape, you may want to have the person who works with you as the client help you in discussing which of the planning exercises were most and least helpful. This will be beneficial to you in thinking about the ways in which you may want to introduce goal setting and planning exercises into your long-term counseling in the future.

Chapter Six **BACK TALK**

Please answer the following questions for this chapter:

I. What is the main point of this chapter? _____

_____

_____

_____

2. What was your favorite illustration/story in this chapter? Why?_____

_____

_____

_____

3. Describe a personal experience you have had as a counselor or counselee (formal or informal) that relates to the content of this chapter:_____

_____

_____

_____

_____

4. What question(s) do you have after reading this chapter?_____

_____

_____

_____

_____

5. What would you like to learn more about in this course?_____

_____

_____

_____

_____

Chapter Six **TAPED INTERVIEW ANALYSIS**

Name: _____

Date: _____

Interview Number: _____

1. What was the client's presenting (initial) problem or opportunity?_____

_____

_____

_____

2. What skills did you attempt to practice in this interview? Give one or more

examples: _____

_____

_____

_____

3. What do you feel you did best in this interview? _____

_____

_____

_____

4. What do you feel you need to improve upon based on this interview? ___

_____

_____

_____

5. Describe any surprises, shifts in direction or content, or significant positive or negative turning points in this interview: _____

_____

_____

_____

6. How was the client thinking and/or feeling by the end of this interview? __

_____

_____

_____

7. If this were an interview series, what do you think might happen in the next interview? _____

_____

_____

_____

8. What did you learn most about the process of personal counseling from conducting this interview? _____

_____

_____

_____

Chapter Six **THE COUNSELOR'S LIBRARY**

Consider adding one or more of these books to your counseling library:

Brother Lawrence. *The Practice of the Presence of God.* Westwood, N.J.: Fleming M. Revell Company, 1958.
> This devotional classic is an example of a man putting his relationship with God above every other value.

Cheydleur, John R. *Linked Commitments.* San Diego: Christian Systems Management, 1979.
> This self-paced seminar includes tapes and workbook pages leading you through the process of developing effective goals and objectives for your own life and ministry.

Covey, Stephen R., with A. Roger Merrill and Rebecca R. Merrill. *First Things First.* New York: Fireside/Simon and Shuster, 1994.
> This book is an extremely helpful guide for developing a planning-and-priority system for business and personal life based on values.

Johnson, Vernon E. *I'll Quit Tomorrow.* San Francisco: Harper and Row, 1980.
> This classic book in the addiction field shows how to do an effective intervention for an addicted person. Four handbooks are included for outpatients, patients, clergymen, and hospital personnel.

Lundy, Jim. *Lead, Follow, or Get Out of the Way.* San Diego: Avant Books, 1986.
> This is an exciting "do-it-now" planner's guide to success, written by a corporate CEO and management consultant. While not totally Christian, there is much to be gleaned from this book about effective goals, objectives, and action.

Morgan, G. Campbell. *The Practice of Prayer.* Westwood, N.J.: Fleming H. Revell Company, undated.
> Dr. Morgan is one of the finest theologians and prayer teachers of the last century. A valuable resource for both counselors and clients.

# PART THREE

# SPECIALTY SKILLS

Doc & Duck © 1999 Andrew J. Cheydleur

# Specialty Scripture Skills

*There is a story about a pastor, faced with one of his deacons who wanted to divorce his wife because, he said, he didn't love her anymore. Thinking rapidly, his pastor challenged the deacon with the Bible's command, "Husbands, love your wives" (Eph. 5:25).*

*Responding just as quickly, the deacon shot back, "But she really isn't my wife anymore; she's moved into a bedroom down the hall, and we haven't even had sex for months!"*

*The pastor's next probe was, "Doesn't that make her your neighbor?" He then confronted the deacon, "Jesus commands us in Matthew 22:39 to 'Love your neighbor as yourself.'"*

*Not convinced by this argument, the deacon snapped back, "But she is mean and spiteful to me, so she really doesn't count as a neighbor!"*

*The pastor thought about this briefly, then prompted, "Doesn't that make her your enemy?" and rammed home the final point with, "The Bible commands us in Matthew 5:44 to 'Love your enemies!'"*

*The pastor won the argument, but he lost the marriage.*

## One-on-One Preaching Is Not Counseling

ONE OF THE GREAT strengths we can bring to the personal counseling process is our ability to use Scripture to help people clarify their values and resolve value conflicts. Because of our commitment to study the Bible and reflect upon our own personal experiences with God, we readily accept the truth of such verses as "The way of the Lord is strength for the upright, but destruction will come to the workers of iniquity" (Prov. 10:29). It doesn't take any stretch of imagination for us to believe that God's goodness will bless those who obey him and that the wicked will eventually find some way to destroy themselves. Likewise, even a more obscure reference, such as Moses' blessing to Asher, "Your sandals shall be iron and bronze; as your days, so shall your strength be" (Deut. 33:25), does not faze us as we want to believe that God is interested in undergirding the stamina and health of the believer.

However, preaching is not counseling. The bright, happy, authoritative way in which we might present a Scripture from the pulpit may be very difficult for a troubled, sad, doubting client to accept and integrate into his/her life. We would certainly accept the premise of Dr. Jay Adams (*Shepherding God's Flock,* 1974), "The Scriptures contain all of the principles that are necessary for meeting the needs of sheep . . . the Bible is the textbook for teaching them how to love God and their neighbors which is what counseling is all about." We are also aware that teaching any new information to a person under stress has its own disciplines and problems even when that information is the Good News that God presents in Scripture.

Although it is very important for us to have a broad and accurate grasp of the Scriptures in order to help people, we might also want to constantly keep before us the wisdom of Proverbs 19:22, "What is desired in a man is kindness," and remember that our tender and loving concern may tell a person more about the character of God the Father than any of the specific biblical texts we provide.

## Process of Spiritual Counseling

---

**SKILL-BUILDER TIP**

In completing the Skill Builders in this chapter, you may find it helpful to use a topical Bible or a Bible-promise book in order to speed your access to appropriate Scriptures. In addition, you may find it helpful to refer to Continuing Education 102 and Continuing Education 103 at the end of this book.

---

*Elizabeth and Dorothy were mothers who worked in the same office. They also attended the same church. Their daughters took tennis lessons together. Then something happened, and Dorothy stopped her daughter's contact with Elizabeth's daughter.*

*At first, Elizabeth was tempted to "strike." After talking with her pastor, she decided that she placed a high value on active forgiveness. Elizabeth developed an anonymous campaign of small items that she gave to Dorothy once a week: a card, a bookmark, a flower, candy, etc. She kept this up until the sense of rejection was gone from her heart. And one year later, Dorothy invited Elizabeth's daughter to a wonderful party with her daughter.*

---

**Chart 7.1 SIMPLE REACTION PATTERN**

I EXPERIENCE ⟶ I FEEL ⟶ I ACT

| | | |
|---|---|---|
| whatever, or whoever, does something to me. | happy, or sad, or angry, etc.... I think that I cannot control or change how I feel. | in a way to minimize pain or maximize pleasure in the short term. |

---

From the client's viewpoint, when a life event is experienced, it causes feelings. The client does the best that he or she can to either maximize the pleasure or reduce the pain of those feelings. Sometimes this automatic process works out in a satisfactory manner.

Often, without spiritual counseling a man or woman is cast on the shoals of life.

---

**Chart 7.2 CONSEQUENCE WITHOUT COUNSELING**

## I SMASH MYSELF
### AGAINST THE REALITIES OF A HARSH LIFE.

---

With appropriate Christian counseling, a more extended sequence of events is experienced. The first two events (experience and emotional reaction) remain the same, but when the spiritual counseling process intervenes, it helps the client examine personal feelings and reactions to find out his or her current (often competing) beliefs and values.

---

**Chart 7.3 ACTION PATTERN WITH COUNSELING**

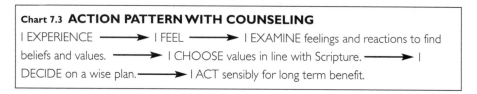

I EXPERIENCE ⟶ I FEEL ⟶ I EXAMINE feelings and reactions to find beliefs and values. ⟶ I CHOOSE values in line with Scripture. ⟶ I DECIDE on a wise plan. ⟶ I ACT sensibly for long term benefit.

---

These beliefs and values are then compared with Scripture in a sensitive and focused way and are either reinforced or revised.

Then, based on the clarity of belief (including the power of prayer), an appropriate decision is made, and an action plan is developed, reinforcing the client's highest values.

---

**Chart 7.4 CONSEQUENCE WITH CHRISTIAN COUNSELING**

## I AM TRANSFORMED
### SO THAT I CAN TRANSFORM REALITY INTO A BETTER LIFE.

---

Action is taken with spiritual accountability, enabling the person to transform his or her circumstances as is appropriate.

## Discover the Content and Emotion First

*While I was consulting with a large and active Christian hot line in Anaheim, California (nine thousand calls per month), one new volunteer counselor picked up a telephone and enthusiastically told the caller, "You must be born again! Jesus is the answer to all your problems." He said this even before he listened to the reason she had called. Imagine his embarrassment when she gently responded through her tears, "I gave my heart to Jesus last week, and now my father has thrown me out of our house."*

Before it is appropriate to apply any Scripture to the client's life, you need to thoroughly explore the content of the situation, the emotions that are connected to the content, and the values that underlie those emotions. As you do this, depend on the Spirit for your leading, using the techniques of empathy and probes that you have practiced. You will want to be listening for the areas in which the client's values are clear and confident and those areas in which the client is fearful or confused.

Psalm 27:1 contains affirmation for the obedient, sane believer: "The Lord is my light and my salvation; whom shall I fear? The Lord is the strength of my life; of whom shall I be afraid?" As you are engaged in the process of discovering the content and emotions of your client, you will begin to pick up important cues about his or her values and belief system. Is this client able to trust the Lord for regular guidance? Does this person depend on the Lord for forgiveness from sin and deliverance from spiritual and temporal problems? Does this person know specific individuals or have areas of life that cause him or her fear? Does this person have a satisfying devotional life, which allows him or her to draw strength from God?

As you are listening and exploring the client's issues from his or her point of view, you will not be asking most of these questions in an outright fashion. Indeed, it would be insensitive and might appear uncaring and rude for you to do so. You begin by focusing on the immediate concerns that the client brings. On the other hand, if you do not listen for the cues, you will not have conducted your exploration at a deep enough level to begin to understand the client's social and spiritual values and value conflicts. These value issues always undergird and influence the client's emotions and thinking.

---

**Skill Builder 7.1**  Practice asking effective spiritual probe questions regarding spiritual issues in the following exercises:

EXAMPLE
*Client:* "I really am trying to pray, but I just don't think that God is listening to my prayers."
*Spiritual Probe:* "How do you feel when God doesn't respond to your prayers?"

PRACTICE
A. *Client:* "I seem to have a nagging sense of guilt about the type of job I am in and the different things that I am required to do if I want to be successful."

*Spiritual Probe Question:* _____

_____

_____

B. *Client:* "I know she is my sister-in-law, but I really don't want her to come live in my house, not even for a weekend."

*Spiritual Probe Question:* _____

_____

_____

---

## Clarify Values and Beliefs

*Mary was the second daughter of a large family. As an adult she chose to stay at home and delay starting her own family in order to take care of her increasingly invalid mother.*

*Discussion with a counselor showed that she did not feel coerced or pressured into the sacrifice she was making. Instead, it proceeded from deep religious and family values.*

*Because her commitment was well thought out and her values were not distorted, she was able to marry and raise her own children after her mother's death without regret about beginning "late in life."*

In your taped practice interview sessions, if you have been carefully attending to the experiences, emotions, and beliefs of your clients, you probably are developing a sense of their perspective. When empathy alone has failed to move an interview forward, you have engaged in appropriate prompts and probes to continue the exploration process.

Because you have used the skills you are learning without neglecting to pray either silently or aloud for the leading of the Spirit in your counseling relationship, the Lord is already beginning to work through you to provide strength to your clients. You are becoming an emotional and spiritual shelter for them, in fulfillment of the Scripture verse "The Lord is their strength, and He is the saving refuge of His anointed" (Ps. 28:8).

It is truly an awesome responsibility to realize, in the midst of a counseling interview, that a client has placed trust and dependency on you. This is almost the same way that you place trust and dependency on God. As you continue in the counseling process, allow the Spirit to lead you in selecting from among the skills you have learned to use. The client's perspective will become increasingly clear. Both you and the client begin to mutually understand the values and beliefs that have shaped that perspective.

---

**Skill Builder 7.2**  In the next two exercises, write a reflection statement that is designed to help clarify the client's perspective; do not attempt to change the client's perspective at this point.

### EXAMPLE
*Client:* "I know you are really not supposed to hit women, and I didn't really want to hit her, but she made me so angry that in a way, I did want to hit her!"
*Reflection Statement:* "So it seems to me your values, and to some extent even your basically decent feelings, are lined up *against* violence toward women, yet for some reason, in this situation, the things she did made you so angry, you almost crossed over the values and boundaries you had set for yourself in this area."

### PRACTICE

A. *Client:* "Pastor, I know Susan just got engaged to Bob last week, but I just can't stop thinking about her—the way she looks, the way her hair blows in the breeze, the way she would feel if she would let me touch her. . . . Pastor, you're a man, you know how it is."

*Reflection Statement:* _____

_____

_____

B. *Client:* "Well, he is really very nice to me, gentle and personable and generous, so I figure that if his wife doesn't like him, there is something wrong with her in the head. I don't see any reason why I shouldn't be able to date him and be happy about the gifts that he gives me. Do you?"

*Reflection Statement:* _____

_____

_____

## Transform Perspective with Scripture

*One of The Salvation Army Adult Rehabilitation Center's administrators was recently asked to referee a dispute between a new convert at the center and another man who was unconverted. The new convert raised the following moral question to The Salvation Army officer. "Andy here says it's OK to pay a woman to have sex, but I was brought up that sex is only moral if you don't have to pay for it. Which of us is right?"*

*The Salvation Army Officer neither laughed at his simplistic thinking nor allowed it to remain unchallenged. Instead, a guided Bible study, using a concordance to locate such phrases as, "he knew her" and "fornication" (simply defined as singles sex), allowed the client to gain and take ownership of a clear, biblically based value set of his own.*

*As the rehabilitation-center convert increasingly sought to guide his sex life and came to grips with biblical standards, the counseling process moved to a decision about those standards. Based on his decision to accept biblical values in this area of his life, he began to develop a new action plan founded on these new values. An accountability group of longer-term converts then supported the action plan that was decided upon.*

As spiritual counselors, we are not satisfied with moving into decision making and action planning based only on the limited or wounded perspective that the client has developed from past life experiences. From a professional standpoint, it would be irresponsible to suggest to a client that past life experiences that have brought him or her to a point of pain, confusion, and difficulty have also, in some magical way, given him or her sufficient resources, wisdom, and spiritual buoyancy to be able to solve his or her problems and plan for the future based solely on the past information that he or she brings to the interview process.

As spiritual counselors, we want the client to have access to all the new information he or she needs to assimilate before making critical decisions and moving to the stage of action planning. Sometimes the new information that a client needs may be specific task information, such as the cost of tuition at various colleges or the time of day a particular welfare office opens.

Very often in our biblically deficient culture, the critical information that a client needs and does not yet have is actually found in the Bible. In some situations you will be using Scripture to support and affirm the values of the client. At other times you will introduce Scripture so that the client can compare and correct his or her contradictory values and misbeliefs.

Often a client will come to you with a confused combination of family traditions, cultural values, folk sayings, and some values that are derived from Scripture, although possibly distorted. In trying to make useful decisions based on this collection of multiple reference points, the client has become confused and at some level "lost his/her way." The task of counseling, then, includes sorting out the sources of some of these deeply ingrained but possibly conflicting values. It also includes providing clear scriptural information against which the various values and beliefs may be tested.

> *One of the counselors-in-training was doing some informal personal counseling with a man who was brought up to despise African-American people. The client stated that he didn't understand why he felt the way he did. Through guided Bible study, he was able to change his former irrational prejudice as he came to understand the dignity and value God places on each individual human life, even while we are still in the womb (Job 10:8; Jer. 1:5).*

Turn to Continuing Education 102, "Scripture-Based Values," to see how specific Scriptures can be used to confront nonbiblical cultural values in the areas of ethics and business, social issues, sex and relationships, expectation and gratitude, and spiritual/emotional values.

The counselor and the client seek together for a transformed perspective. The goal is to have the client's value system become deeply penetrated by the truth of God. Then his or her emotions and subconscious attitudes can "track" along with the conscious decisions of his or her mind. Most people would like to feel strong and powerful and have things go well. However, they are continually sabotaged by competing values that interfere with each other, sometimes just below the surface of conscious awareness. In order for these values to line up in the same direction so that the subconscious tracks where the conscious mind directs, the person must have a transformed perspective. The desires of the heart must be based on the good desires God has for him or her.

The Scripture actually holds the promise of personal stability as stated in 2 Samuel 22:33-34: "God is my strength and power, and He makes my way perfect. He makes my feet like the feet of deer, and sets me on my high places." The reference in this Scripture is to the mountain deer, who can travel the narrow ledges without falling because its back feet step in the exact same position where its front feet have already safely tested the ledges. Similarly, a person whose narcissistic perspective is opened up to a godly perspective is able to make important quality-of-life decisions and have his or her subconscious mind support those kinds of decisions.

 **Skill Builder 7.3** In these exercises we want to move from clarifying the client's perspective to the step of beginning to transform the client's perspective through the use of Scripture. Notice we (a) start by reflecting the highest value the client expresses, then (b) state a correcting or affirming Scripture, then (c) reflect the client's possible feeling about the Scripture.

### EXAMPLE
*Client:* "Well, pastor, I think I am a mostly moral person according to the Bible, but I don't know if I can put up with all this stuff my wife is bringing home from the Bible study about spiritual guidance and miracles and divine intervention and everything."

*Introducing Transformational Scripture:* "(a) So what I am getting here is you take pretty strong responsibility for your own actions. You even base those actions on biblical ethics, but (b) a Scripture like that passage in the book of Daniel, chapter 5, where there is handwriting on the wall put there by God and Daniel interprets it, (c) would be kind of tough for you to swallow. It seems as though God is doing something Daniel is not really having full control over. Would that be about right?"

### PRACTICE
A. *Client:* "I don't know exactly how to say this, counselor, but I feel OK about coming to the Lord to pray to have my sins forgiven, but I don't know if I even think its right for me, or maybe for anybody else, to ask him to help with, you know, material things, like getting a car that works or the raise in my salary I need, or anything that, you know, actually helps me personally."

*Reflect client's highest value:* (a) _____

_____

_____

*State Scripture* (b) _____

_____

_____

*Reflect client's feeling* (c) _____

_____

B. *Client:* "Well we really showed them, didn't we, Pastor? I mean, nobody thought we could raise enough money for the new Sunday school wing when you made me chairman of the fund drive, but we pulled it off! And I feel really good about it!"

*Reflect client's highest value:* (a) _____

_____

*State Scripture* (b) _____

_____

Reflect client's feeling (c)_____

_____

Each interview and/or series of counseling interviews allows us to explore a client's values more deeply. It is important that the client and the counselor mutually achieve some measure of a "transformed perspective," or at least a biblically affirmed perspective (if a client's perspective is fairly close to biblical values). This perspective shift or validation should occur prior to significant decision making or action planning.

## Scripture As Unique Information

> When a young woman shoplifter, referred by the court, came to me with sin and confusion in a number of areas of her life, each area needed to be examined and dealt with before she could achieve a stable Christian life. However, if I had started by telling her that she needed to obey all of the Ten Commandments (found in Exodus 20), I could have pushed her away from me and my premature counseling. A more focused confrontation, properly timed and based specifically upon the commandment "You shall not steal" (Exod. 20:15), was received as more penetrating, more healing, and less condemning.

As Gerard Egan points out in his skill-development manual *Exercises in Helping Skills,* "Sometimes clients do not get a clear picture of a problem situation because they are not aware that they lack information needed for clarity. Information can provide clients with some of the new perspectives they need to see problem situations as manageable. However, note that giving clients problem-clarifying information or helping them find it themselves is not the same as advice giving. Furthermore, information giving is not to be confused with clichés or amateur philosophizing." The introduction of Scripture into your counseling process is a very specific, focused form of information giving and should not be taken lightly or done casually.

In a sense, preaching is a "shotgun" approach to problem solving, in which a basic scriptural truth is presented to a congregation. The speaker hopes that the "shot" will somehow hit some of the specific needs that the congregation has on that day. We all can believe in a general way that God is the one who protects, delivers, and saves the believer, "The Lord is my rock and my fortress and my deliverer; my God, my strength, in whom I will trust" (Ps. 18:2). However, the introduction of such scriptural truths into the individual counseling process cannot be done the same way as in preaching.

Instead, the use of the Bible in counseling must be done as a "rifle" approach. Scripture is introduced when it is specifically relevant to the already expressed needs, issues, or value conflicts presented by the client. In the pastoral counseling context, scriptural confrontation may still be quite appropriate, so long as it is extremely specific. Of course, being precise sharpens the penetration power of the confrontation. It also makes it able to be received with less pain because it does not come against as broad an area of the client's previously held values or beliefs. The reference list at the end of this chapter will help identify topical Scripture-based resources that can be used to focus your use of Scripture in counseling.

It is certainly true that God wants to save his people and bless their inheritance (Ps. 28:9). The same verse also reminds us that God does the specific work of "shepherding them" as individuals with specific needs, individual confusion, and personalized desires for guidance and/or correction. That Scripture also says God will "bear them up forever," so He does not try to force an issue with His people due to any lack of patience on His part. We, as faith-based counselors, must have the same patience with both our clients and ourselves. We cannot settle for a "blunderbuss" scriptural approach that is too general to precisely fit the situation. Thoughtful prayer and Bible study help us to be more specific with our application of Scripture and less painful and frightening.

---

**Skill Builder 7.4** Add to your inventory of Scriptures suitable for use in counseling. Look up the following Scriptures which are specifically related to human emotions. Mark them in your Bible, or begin to index them on your computer for future reference.

❑ *Anger:* Psalm 30:5; Psalm 37:8; Proverbs 14:17; Proverbs 15:1; Proverbs 15:18; Proverbs 19:3

❑ *Hurt:* Psalm 25:3; Matthew 5:10; Matthew 5:44; Matthew 6:14; 2 Corinthians 4:8-9; Ephesians 4:31

❑ *Sadness:* Psalm 145:14; Isaiah 53:4; John 16:20; Romans 8:16-18; 2 Corinthians 4:17

❑ *Uselessness:* Matthew 10:42; 2 Corinthians 5:18; Galatians 4:6-7; Ephesians 2:10; 1 John 3:2; 1 Peter 2:9

❑ *Worry:* Psalm 4:8; Psalm 32:7; Psalm 55: 22; Isaiah 26:3; Matthew 6:30; Philippians 4:19

❑ *Loneliness:* Psalm 46:1; Psalm 55:22; Psalm 68:6; Psalm 147:3; John 14:18; 1 Peter 5:7

❑ *Powerlessness:* Deuteronomy 33:25; Psalm 18:2; Proverbs 3:26; Isaiah 40:29; Isaiah 40:30-31

### Searching for Scriptural Information

But what if you don't know the right Scripture? Dr. Adams says:

> *It is true that many ministers have not been taught to counsel biblically. Moreover, the art of counseling improves not as information is acquired but as skills are developed; these are not all attained all at once and, in particular, not gained apart from doing. So then, what (should you do, when you do) not know what to do? The answer to that is simple (but not necessarily easy). First, (the counselor) says so, "frankly, I am stymied about some aspects of the problem and I want to spend this next week praying and thinking about the question in light of the Scriptures; I hope you will pray too". Secondly, during the week between counseling sessions he does just that. He pores over the Scriptures to discover God's answers. He dare not fail to do so when he has promised. By the next session, hopefully, in most instances he will have mended his net (and he himself will have grown).*

Shepherding God's Flock, *page 174*

All new information, which challenges the person at a deep level, must be assumed to be difficult to digest emotionally. Therefore, new information should be presented in the form of an "empathy sandwich," as has been discussed previously. The top layer (or first statement) reflects the client's intent and feelings; the second layer (or information statement) presents the new material to the client, and the third layer (or final statement) acknowledges the client's anticipated emotional reaction. The counselor will not assume that any new information, particularly Scripture, has been uncritically accepted and internalized by the client. Information is not personalized simply because the counselor has handed out a book or quoted some words. Instead, the information must be carefully and professionally transmitted.

Deep respect must be shown for the content of information and the dignity of the individual receiving it.

As believers, we are thoroughly convinced that God saves us to become righteous and that he provides us suffi-cient strength to get through the difficult times of our life. We are people called to be spiritual counselors. We know God has delegated authority to us and holds us responsible for being His agents to fulfill such promises as Psalm 37:39-40 for those whom we serve: "But the salvation of the righteous is from the Lord; He is their strength in the time of trouble. And the Lord shall help them and deliver them." For us to fulfill this great calling and commission, we must make a deep commitment to transmitting the wisdom of God, as found in the Bible, in the most clear, accurate, and appropriate way possible. See Contin-uing Education 102 and 103 for selected Bible verses that can be used in identifying specific scriptural values and potential cultural conflicts.

 **Skill Builder 7.5** In these two exercises, select an appropriate response Scripture and wrap it up in an empathy sandwich. As in Skill Builder 7.3, we want to create an empathy sandwich to (a) reflect the client's content and feeling, (b) quote the Scripture, and (c) reflect the anticipated emotional reaction of the client to the Scripture.

### EXAMPLE

*Client:* "It seems like ever since he has been to that revival meeting, my husband is getting so pushy about this personal God thing! I mean, I have been to church most of my life, and I think church is a good thing to go to, but I have never gotten fanatical about being religious. I mean, you don't have to get all wild-eyed and emotional to be a Christian, do you?"

*Scriptural Empathy Sandwich:* "(a) From what you said earlier, I gather you are happy with the changes in your husband's behavior since he went to the revival meetings. I get the sense now that you are worried he wants you to be some-how different than you are. You are not sure whether being a church attender is enough to really be a complete Christian. On the other hand, you don't want to become some kind of emotional freak. (b) Of course, the Bible is full of passages that remind us that we have an individual will and the ability to choose to follow God or not to follow God. Look at Joshua 24:15, where

Joshua challenged the Jewish people to 'choose for yourselves this day whom you will serve.' The New Testament does get pretty personal with us with teachings from Jesus like John 3:3, 'Unless one is born again, he cannot see the kingdom of God.' (c) I guess that these kinds of personalized Scripture verses might make you uncomfortable at this point. Your background is pretty much being in the church, but not really being able to point to a personal time or place of decision about Jesus Christ."

PRACTICE

A. *Client:* "I don't really get all this stuff about trying to hear God's voice by reading the Bible and all that sort of baloney. I don't want to be irreverent or anything, but it seems to be a pretty big leap of faith to put all your trust in one book. I really don't see that God has much to do with telling me how I should run my life."

*Scriptural Empathy Sandwich:* (a) _____

_____

(b)_____

_____

(c)_____

_____

B. *Client:* "It isn't exactly that I don't believe in God, and I think the prayers they say in church are all right, but I think I would be pretty afraid to share any of my own thoughts or emotions with God, because I don't really think He gives a rip about me!"

*Scriptural Empathy Sandwich:* (a) _____

_____

(b)_____

_____

(c)_____

_____

## Providing Confidence

*As one young minister-in-training related his experience of being a client, "The Lord spoke to me, as I was being counseled, when the counselor pointed out*

*2 Corinthians 1:4." This verse states that "God comforts us . . . that we may be able to comfort those who are in any trouble, with the comfort with which we ourselves are comforted by God." He continued, "It was then I responded to the 'call' to be a minister."*

We know God provides confidence to us as believers: "For the Lord will be your confidence, and will keep your foot from being caught" (Prov. 3:26). Similarly, we want to be so dependable in our use of Scripture that clients will allow us to be their confidence, at least as it relates to the issues of the counseling process. They can trust us to keep them from being caught up in any kind of error, either one that they bring to the counseling session and

that we fail to confront or any misinterpretation or exaggeration of Scripture on our part.

In order for this confidence not to be misplaced, our use of the Bible must cleanly contrast or clearly reinforce the scriptural value that relates to the personal or cultural values about which the client is concerned.

When the Scripture that is being presented is in contrast or contradiction to a personal or cultural value already held by the client, it is extremely important we not overstate the case for Scripture. Instead, we allow the Word of God to do its own work in the person's heart. It is unethical and will also cause great damage to the counseling relationship for us to overdramatize a biblical passage. Also, we do not imply things from the Scripture that are not supported by the context in which the Bible itself presents a verse.

It is professionally and spiritually appropriate for us to present the Scripture accurately, forcibly, and clearly so that the client can compare his or her current value with the competing or confirming value, as presented by God in the Bible. Then, we must somehow "stand back" emotionally from the decision the client makes and allow him or her the same dignity God allows us—to be wrong, to suffer consequences, and to repent at some future date. This is so even though we will not personally receive any ego satisfaction or glory from the client's transformation at that time. As Paul pointed out in his letter to the Corinthians, "So then neither he who plants is anything, nor he who waters, but God who gives the increase" (1 Cor. 3:7). You have not failed if you have properly done the work of counseling, even if the client makes a bad decision. Your responsibility is to see that informed choice is made clearly, with accurate biblical and other necessary information. The

Word of God will never return void but will always do the work of power that God has sent it to do.

When the Scripture is clearly presented and you surround it with an appropriate empathy sandwich, you should still allow the client to verbalize some indecisiveness while he or she is going through the process of decision. If you do not hear any verbalization of this process of decision, then you may suspect the client is being "passive" in order to please you rather than doing the actual work of decision making.

In order for you to sense the process is working properly, you should hear the client verbalize any indecisiveness. Be prepared to be empathetic rather than allowing yourself to be impatient by asking him or her to "get on with it" in some rapid-fire way.

Having worked through the indecisiveness to the point of a decision, you should expect to have the client clearly verbalize the decision, one way or another, that he or she has made between competing values.

**Skill Builder 7.6** Answer the following questions and requests about spiritual information in a way that first (a) restates the client's question; then (b) provides information that is accurate, confident, and consistent with Scripture; and finally (c) invites a specific response to the Scripture by the client.

EXAMPLE

*Client:* "Pastor, now that I have become a Christian, it seems to me that everything in my past, present, and future is forgiven, so there really isn't anything a Christian can do anymore that is actually sin, is there?"

*Response:* "(a—restatement) I am not quite sure from your question whether you're asking whether forgiveness covers all sins, or whether there just simply aren't any sins that God sees in a Christian, but (b—information) it might be helpful for you to read some of the book of Galatians, particularly chapter 5, beginning at verse 18, where Paul discusses the difference between being led by the Spirit and having the deeds of the flesh, which are still under the law. This passage lists a number of actions that are described as the deeds of the flesh, including immorality, idolatry, sorcery, drunkenness, and a number of others. Further down in this passage, in verse 22, the actions and attitudes that are the fruit of the Spirit are also listed. (c—invitation) Perhaps you would like to meditate on these two lists and come back and talk to me about which of your actions fit on which of the lists and how you can grow spiritually to develop the fruit of the Spirit."

PRACTICE

A. *Client:* "Counselor, I would really like to have God heal some of my emotional scars from the past, but my friend Pam says that emotional healing doesn't have anything to do with God. What do you think?"

*Response:*

a. (restatement): _____

_____

b. (information): _____

_____

c. (invitation): _____

_____

B. *Client:* "I don't think anybody at all should have to go through what my father did to me! I don't think people are fair, and I don't think God is fair if I'm going to be judged for what I've done, and he gets off scot-free!"

*Response:*

a. (restatement): _____

_____

b. (information): _____

_____

c. (invitation): _____

_____

## Respecting Client Values, Decisions, and Action Plans

When your client clearly states his or her decision, you empathize by clearly reflecting the content, emotion, and value components that went into that decision. This does not necessarily mean you agree with the decision but that you hear it and respect it and that you respect the client and accord him or her the dignity of the decision-making responsibility. Another reason you restate the decision is to check for accuracy in hearing the decision and check for the client's commitment to the decision.

If you have accurately heard the client's decision and he or she seems to be truly committed to it, then the Spirit should be giving both you and your client a measure of peace: "The Lord will bless His people with peace" (Ps. 29:11). If you are receiving this sense of peace together, then you can expect the first part of that same verse to be true, "The Lord will give strength to His people. "

If either you or the client does not have a sense of spiritual peace about the decision, then the two of you should not proceed at this point! Instead, you need to back up the counseling process. Return to previously discussed areas. You may have possibly missed the client's concern or failed to be accurate enough in the use of Scripture or other needed information. It is also possible you may need to find places where the client has deliberately lied or inadvertently misled you. He or she may have omitted some key facts or failed to reveal an important emotion or blocking value.

In our fast-paced society, we, like our clients, have been conditioned to expect rapid results. Rapid results are wonderful, even miraculous, when they occur. However, when they don't occur, it is unprofessional, unethical, and downright absurd to push for premature closure when it doesn't really exist. As Dr. David Stoop phrases it, "Don't push the river."

If the decision reached about values is accurate and you and the counselee both feel the peace of God, then together you can apply the value decision to the particular problem at hand. Then begin to think about action planning. At this point one helpful scriptural approach is the use of the parables of Christ, which have a way of eliciting creativity and possibilities from the client.

The area of action planning is more fully discussed in chapter 6, which shows several ways to complete the counseling interview or the interview series through actions that provide a platform for future growth.

---

**Skill Builder 7.7** Clearly restate the following value-linked client decisions, using your own paraphrases of their statements.

EXAMPLE

*Client:* "I know God wants me to forgive my neighbor for chopping down the tree on the border between our two properties, but I just can't bring myself to do it yet."

*Restatement:* "So you have come to the point where you're pretty clear on what God wants you to do regarding this incident with the tree, which is really to forgive your neighbor for chopping it down. . . . But somehow you just seem to need to hold on to the resentment for a while longer before you can give it over to God."

PRACTICE

A. *Client:* "I think I've really decided if I ever want to be a married, Christian woman, I am going to first have to give up this sexual relationship with my boss, even if it means I lose my job. I don't really think I should even see him socially again, so I will go into the office Monday morning and tell him that it won't be continuing anymore."

*Restatement:* So you . . . _____

_____

_____

B. *Client:* "Well, pastor, I know you think I shouldn't gamble, but I don't think you have yet proven it to me from the Bible. We haven't actually lost the house yet, so I think I am planning to go to the racetrack Saturday to see if I can win the big one!"

*Restatement:* So you . . . _____

_____

_____

## Principles for Introducing Scripture

Scripture can be presented in such a way that it is internalized by the client and becomes helpful in forming a transformed perspective. This forms a basis for deep-level decision making and effective action planning. Three things must be taken into account:

First, before transmitting Scripture, the counselor must clearly recognize and verbally reflect the values the client holds. Later, these may require scriptural affirmation or require the introduction of new Scripture for clarification or confrontation.

The material in chapters 4 and 5 is designed to strengthen your skills in this vital area.

Unless the client's values are clearly recognized by the counselor and the Scripture selected is as specific as possible in relation to the value issues under consideration, the Scripture will "fall on deaf ears." It will fail to be utilized, or, worse, the introduction of the Bible will drive a wedge between the counselor and the client, possibly hurting the sense of empathy and relationship that is critical to the counseling process.

Second (it may seem simple, but it is not), the counselor must know how to find the appropriate Scripture to apply to the situation and/or value conflict. This means that a person who aspires to be a faith-based counselor must sufficiently discipline him- or herself to learn enough about the Bible. This knowledge should be tied to a variety of common counseling topics, emotions, and value issues, so they will have a reasonable set of tools from which to select when the need arises. Unfortunately, many otherwise excellently prepared Christian social workers, psychologists, and family therapists do not have an undergraduate background of Biblical training. Having such a background would give them the broad access to Scripture they need for their counseling clients.

An introduction to the use of Scripture to sort out biblical norms from common cultural values is provided in Continuing Education 102, "Scripture-Based Values." Continuing Education 103, "Topical Scripture References," lists additional Bible verses that are related to common counseling topics. In addition, a number of helpful Scripture-based tools for the spiritual counselor are described in the "The Counselor's Library" section at the end of this chapter.

Third, the introduction of Scripture, as with the introduction of any new information, should always be assumed to be emotionally threatening to the client, no matter how helpful it may ultimately prove to be. To reduce the client's emotional reaction, Scripture should usually be introduced in an empathy sandwich. The client's content, emotions, and values are caringly and accurately reflected to him or her prior to the introduction of the new scriptural material. After the scriptural material has been inserted, the reverse side of the empathy sandwich needs to be applied, in which the client's emotions and potential reactions are caringly and appropriately framed by the pastoral counselor.

It is very easy for us to get so caught up in the intellectual search for new biblical information or in the emotional enthusiasm of transmitting this new information that we fail to maintain these critical disciplines. They should be observed every time new scriptural material is introduced to a client.

The Skill Builders for this chapter are designed to strengthen your ability to connect Scripture with counseling issues in a focused way. In doing these exercises, you will want to work with a topical reference Bible, such as the *Thompson Chain Reference Bible* or *Dake's Bible.* If your Bible background is more limited, you may want to begin by using a Bible-promise book that is indexed in relation to emotions, such as *God's Promises for Your Every Need* (Countryman/Ward/Nelson, 1995) or *The Living Bible Promise Book* (Barbour Books, 1988).

Prepare to conduct and tape-record your next practice interview. When conducting this interview, have a Bible or a Scripture Promise Book with you in the interview so that you and your client can refer to it easily in relation to specific value questions that may come up in the interview.

Continue to pay close attention to the way you understand your client's values and relate those values to those in the Bible. Maintain your own ability to provide accurate empathy to the client even when difficult value issues are being explored.

When you later review this tape, make notes of the way in which the Bible was used appropriately, or misapplied, or was not able to be applied because you did not know the particular passage you needed.

Chapter Seven **BACK TALK**

Please answer the following questions for this chapter:

1. What is the main point of this chapter? _____

_____

_____

2. What was your favorite illustration/story in this chapter? Why? _____

_____

_____

3. Describe a personal experience you have had as a counselor or counselee (formal or informal) that relates to the content of this chapter: _____

_____

_____

4. What question(s) do you have after reading this chapter? _____

_____

_____

5. What would you like to learn more about in this course? _____

_____

_____

Chapter Seven **TAPED INTERVIEW ANALYSIS**

Name: _____

Date: _____

Interview Number: _____

1. What was the client's presenting (initial) problem or opportunity? _____

_____

_____

2. What skills did you attempt to practice in this interview? Give one or more examples: _____

_____

_____

3. What do you feel you did best in this interview? _____

_____

_____

4. What do you feel you need to improve upon based on this interview? ___

_____

_____

5. Describe any surprises, shifts in direction or content, or significant positive or negative turning points in this interview: _____

_____

_____

6. How was the client thinking and/or feeling by the end of this interview? __

_____

_____

7. If this were an interview series, what do you think might happen in the next interview?_____

_____

_____

8. What did you learn most about the process of personal counseling from conducting this interview? _____

_____

_____

Consider adding one or more of these books to your counseling library:

Adams, Jay E. *Competent to Counsel*. Grand Rapids: Baker Book House, 1970.
This is the book that single-handedly started the back-to-the-Bible pastoral-counseling movement! Some antipsychology polemic but a must-read for every Christian counselor.

Gill, A. L. *God's Promises for Your Every Need*. Dallas: Countryman/Ward/ Nelson, 1995
This is a well-structured promise book that comes in both an inexpensive "giveaway" paperback version and an attractive leather-bound version. I particularly like sections 4, 5, and 6, which organize Scriptures by feelings, struggles, and life problems.

*The Living Bible Promise Book*. Uhrichsville, Ohio: Barbour Books, 1988.
This is a nice, pocket-sized promise book with Bible verses sorted into many categories from "food" to "forgiveness." The Living Bible text makes it very readable, and the price makes it available as a gift item for clients.

Reference Bibles: Consistent favorites among pastoral counselors of various persuasions have been *The Thompson Chain Reference Bible* (Kirkbridge Bible Company), *The Ryrie Study Bible* (Moody Press), *Dake's Bible* (Dake's Bible Company), and *The Life Application Bible* (Tyndale House).

Strong, James. *Strong's Exhaustive Concordance of the Bible*. New York: Abingdon Press, 1890/1965.
Every pastoral counselor needs this resource some time, which indexes every word in the King James Bible! Since it is now in public domain, this massive reference work can be inexpensively purchased.

*The Word in Life Study Bible* (N.T.). Nashville: Thomas Nelson, 1993.
One of the most modern format study Bibles on the market, this Bible's style is so topical, it feels like you're reading the **New York Post** or **USA Today**! The "consider this" feature relates Scripture to the practical issues of daily living. A good choice for clients who are new to the use of Scripture.

Doc & Duck © 1999 Andrew J. Cheydleur

# Specialty Prayer Skills

*I was raised in a good, solid, Episcopalian family, where rationality, decency, integrity, and self-sufficiency were the order of the day. The handicap, for a beginning counselor, that resulted from being raised in such a rational and orderly environment was a lack of apparent need for, and therefore a lack of acquaintance with, the positive reality of supernatural faith and miracles.*

PRAYER CAN BE used or misused in counseling. Many important counseling issues are resolved without supernatural intervention. When the client's content and emotion have been "married" together to promote understanding, and his or her underlying personal and cultural values have been explored and compared with biblical values, much of the spiritual work of counseling has already been accomplished.

However, these explorations must ultimately result in actions that change the situation: getting a job, selecting a marriage partner, learning to be assertive on the job, joining AA.

## The "Problem" of Miracles

*John Wimber, who became pastor of the five-thousand-member Vineyard Christian Fellowship, taught a groundbreaking course entitled "Signs and Wonders in Church Growth" at Fuller Seminary in Pasadena, California. A number of young theologians, with backgrounds similar to mine, personally experienced miracles within the classroom in a way for which their own culture had not prepared them. The seminary was in shock and did not know whether this was one of the best courses ever offered or something that should be immediately outlawed in order to restore the orderly academic process.*

Sometimes the change that is desired will require divine intervention along with or in place of planned human action. This is when the prayer for (natural or supernatural) miracles may become an important part of the spiritual counseling process.

Of course, your own family and church background may make it either easy or difficult for you to introduce prayer into your process of counseling.

If you come from the same kind of background as I, you might find it the most difficult and challenging area of your counseling ministry.

Counselors like myself, raised in a Western "rational" culture, may need an extended period of reacculturation in order to accept the miracles some of our clients share with us. Such reacculturation is particularly important if we are to be able to join our clients in believing for future miracles.

Of course, some preachers have emphasized the demonstration of miracles in their public ministries for years. They have dramatized the interruption of the natural order by God in a way that has been helpful to many in building faith but that has also resulted in others' going away disappointed. The task of the spiritual counselor, working in the arena of the supernatural, is to be a rational and wise guide for the counselee while working in an area often reacted to as emotional and unpredictable.

This chapter looks at four areas in which understanding the supernatural may be relevant to the process of counseling.

1. Helping the healing process
2. Counseling persons who have low expectations of God
3. Working through problems in prayer
4. Developing prayer disciplines as a spiritual counselor

Throughout the next two chapters, the most important thing you can do in your training as a counselor is to note and process your own feelings as you visit several of the areas of the supernatural. Note where you find yourself comfortable and where you find yourself uncomfortable. Also, note any areas in which you have an unhealthy and dramatic need to be overly accepting or rejecting of reported supernatural phenomena. Your personal interest, or lack thereof, should not interfere with your responsibility to act as a rational guide and counselor in the area of the supernatural.

👋 **Skill Builder 8.1** Please answer the following questions:

A. Have you ever had a specific answer to prayer? If so, describe the circumstances, the prayer, the answer, and your feelings about the answer:_____

_____

_____

_____

B. Have you ever prayed a prayer that was important to you but seemed to remain unanswered or had a disappointing response? If so, describe the circumstances, the prayer, the answer, and your feelings about it: _____

_____

_____

_____

C. Have you ever experienced (for yourself or another person) a situation that you would label as a miracle? If so, describe the general situation, the miraculous intervention, and your feelings about it then and now: _____

_____

_____

_____

## Healing, Not Hurting

*I was called to minister to the family of a pastor who had had a brief adulterous relationship with a woman on his church staff. His parishioners, who loved him, were not willing to put him out of the ministry. They did, however, remove him from the position of senior pastor for a period of more than a year while he and his wife sought marriage counseling and worked on bringing healing to their family.*

*The pastor was also required to privately confess his sin to a number of pastors in his area, one at a time. In order to have future accountability, he also had to publicly acknowledge his sin to the adults in the congregation at a special meeting. This was a very healing church, and the pastor was able to return to his pulpit after experiencing true healing and accountability.*

*Toward the end of this process, an evangelist came to town who was known to do prayers for physical healing. The pastor had a baby daughter who was born with one foot turned outward. The orthopedic specialist indicated that at some point surgery would have to be performed if she were to be able to walk straight without limping. The pastor, who only a year earlier had been ready to desert his wife and children for a new relationship, decided to take the baby to a healing meeting. The visiting evangelist asked if there was anyone else who wanted to receive prayer. At the risk of loss of dignity and disappointment if nothing positive occurred, he brought forward his sleeping baby daughter to the front of the chapel. The evangelist very gently laid his hands on her, anointed her with oil, and prayed for the foot. The pastor returned to his seat with the sleeping baby in his arms. When their daughter awakened the next morning, the pastor's wife went to take the baby out of the crib and noticed that the once-deformed leg had straightened during the night!*

*There is a time for public rejoicing and a time for private contemplation of the awe and mystery of God. For this pastor to receive such a unique sign of healing from God after he had transgressed all the rules that he had preached to other people was not something to dramatically announce from the housetops but something to humbly accept with deep gratitude and a sense of forgiveness and restoration.*

*One could hardly say that the miracle just described was psychological in nature, suggestive, or, from a psychological standpoint, the kind of thing we might call an hysterical conversion reaction. The child was too young to be aware of the words of the prayer at a conscious level.*

*Over and over again, we see spiritual, psychological, and even physical restorations when, through extended and sensitive Christian counseling, people have prepared their hearts to receive blessing by working through the resistances they have toward the love of God.*

From a counseling point of view, there are many kinds of healing. One of the most common we think about in the church is the healing of the spirit through the renewal and restoration of one's spiritual life and relationship with God. In this sense the forgiveness of sins is the agent of the deepest kind of spiritual healing. However, forgiveness of sins is not the only kind of healing with which the church needs to be acquainted. If our spirits or souls become sick because of our own sin, our emotions may become sick because of the sin of other people acting against us. One contribution of psychology to the church is the reminder that many people are continuing to experience hurts that were inflicted on them by others, resulting in a need for emotional healing.

Then there is the healing of the body. Most physical sickness is organic in origin, although some physical symptoms are thought to have major psychological factors. As Christian counselors, we are also open to looking for the spiritual factors that may be present even in physical disease. As discussed in the next chapter, there are those people who are in some way "demonized," and need healing through deliverance. We are certainly aware of many kinds of relationships that need healing and restoration.

Is healing something that often takes place in the snap of a finger, as the positive optimists among us want to believe? Are there some things for which no healing is possible at all, as the cautious pessimists among us might presume?

It is important for us as counselors to remember that some clients may need time to explore and admit their woundedness before being ready to forgive those who have sinned against them. They also need time to experience the emotions of anger, loss, and hurt. The purpose of experiencing anger, loss, and hurt is not for its own sake but to identify those sins against the client that must be forgiven for the healing process to be thorough.

Of course, when behavior is excused rather than forgiven, it tends to repeat itself, whether it is the offense of the client or an offense toward the client. The liberating purpose of forgiveness is not always to restore a relationship but to free the victim from the mental, emotional, and spiritual control of the one who has sinned against him or her. The dual action of acknowledging evil and then offering forgiveness helps to create an emotional boundary against violations by the original perpetrator and against similar violations by others.

Therefore, as counselors, we need to constantly check our own motives. Are we trying to tie up an interview quickly or avoid having the pain of the client contact our own pain? Or are we willing to stand with the client, in the midst of pain, until true healing actually takes place both psychologically and spiritually?

The need for repentance, with which the world of psychology is sometimes uncomfortable, is sometimes the critical factor in preparing people to receive the healing power of God for themselves or their families. Repentance is not simply the act of abandoning a specific sin. It is an internal change of mind and direction. This is often a prerequisite to a stable, outward change of action and lifestyle.

However, your client's need may not be to repent of a specific sin but to repent of the sin of judging God over the disappointments and tragedies of life. The outstanding biblical example of this is found in the book of Job, but there are many examples in contemporary life among our clients.

*A male supervisor for the Bell Telephone Company had gone through young adulthood with a deformed hip. He had to wear a built-up shoe and was unable to participate in gym classes. Although he became professionally successful, his bitterness of spirit served to sabotage his marriage and many other relationships. He did not become a Christian until midlife, when he experienced a degree of forgiveness and acceptance from God that he had not anticipated.*

*Following his conversion, he experienced love and acceptance through the members of various prayer and Bible study groups. At one point he experienced healing prayer within one of those groups, which resulted in his deformed hip being straightened to the point where he no longer had to wear the built-up shoe. He was even able to take up a number of physically demanding sports, including mountain climbing, which he had never been able to do before.*

*While some spiritually minded people would believe in the miracle but not look for its cause, it seems to me from a counseling perspective that it was, first, his reconciliation with God and then, secondly, his reconciliation with himself through the acceptance and love of the members of the various prayer groups with which he was involved that actually set the stage for his body, mind, and spirit to receive the healing that subsequently occurred.*

*For the people who were involved in the prayer group who prayed for his hip, the healing genuinely was instant (within a forty-five-minute prayer period.) However, this spectacular healing may be seen within the larger context of several years of acceptance and prayer that he experienced prior to the healing.*

*In an interview, he also indicated to me that over the years since he experienced the healing, he has made it a point to periodically check his spiritual inventory if he feels any twinge of pain or difficulty in his hip joint.*

Life is complex. The body, mind, and spirit are complex. As counselors, it is not our job to "force" any artificial standard of faith or healing on our clients. It is our role to come alongside them, to be supportive in their ambitions for healing, and to help them sort through all of the various issues that may be involved in healing the hurts they have experienced from life. Ultimately, we help our clients to come into agreement with God about the healing He has already prescribed for them.

---

**Skill Builder 8.2** Briefly list any personal experiences you have had, or experiences that individuals close to you have had, with the following:

A. Positive experiences concerning physical healing: _____

_____

_____

_____


B. Negative experiences concerning physical healing: _____

_____

_____

_____

## Persons with Low Expectations of God

*One brilliant archeologist, a specialist in South American antiquities, told me
he could show me archeological sites in South and North America that proved
that the global trading indicated in the Old Testament actually occurred.
Dr. Courtney still was not willing to believe in a good God, because he was
deformed from polio, which he had as a child. He couldn't believe a good and
fair God would have allowed this to occur. Obviously, his intellect led him
toward God, because his specialty was in an area of science that tended to prove
the authenticity of the Bible, but his damaged emotions would not allow him to
believe, because he had been so harmed as a child by this invasive disease.*

In spiritual counseling it is quite common to find people, even those who
have basic Christian beliefs, whose life experiences have damaged their
ability to pray in faith or to believe that God wants to do anything good for
them beyond "bare bones" salvation.

InterVarsity Press
publishes a marvelous
series of recovery-
oriented Bible studies
that help Christians
recovering in the
areas of abuse, addic-
tions, bitterness,
codependency,
depression, family
dysfunctions, and
other important
concerns. Perhaps the most remarkable booklet in this series is entitled
*Recovery from Distorted Images of God.* It is probably true that more people
have developed their image of God based on their early childhood
parenting experiences than on any particular church theology or doctrinal
system. The child whose father was a remote, cerebral college professor
may grow up to believe God is also remote, uncaring, and unapproachable.
The child whose mother was chaotic, emotionally unpredictable, sometimes warm, and not even physically present at other times may grow up
to believe God does care, and even does miracles, but there isn't any way
to figure out when and where these strange and wonderful events happen.
Then there are those children who grow up believing God is primarily
interested in punishing them. Some continue to believe this lie even as
adults. There are also those adults whose childhood experiences lead them

to believe that "God doesn't love me." There are others who believe that God "can't accept me" or "doesn't want me."

Childhood experiences or problems in later life may result in a person's blaming God as the author of bad things in his or her life. He or she may not examine the fact that the bad things that are occurring in his or her life may be natural consequences of the person's own sinful or unthoughtful acts, the acts of others, satanic activity, physical laws, or even random chance.

---

### ✋ Skill Builder 8.3

A. Briefly describe your own parents' attitudes and practices of discipline, morality, prayer, and forgiveness toward you when you were young: _____

_____

_____

_____

B. Briefly compare your own feelings and attitudes toward God with the way your parents dealt with you as a child: _____

_____

_____

_____

---

In extended counseling, people are often able to work through their unnatural and unfounded attitudes toward God (unfounded and unnatural because they are not natural to the relationship that should exist between the human and God, and they are not founded upon the truth of who God is). Such attitudes may often be founded upon early childhood relationships or tragic life experiences.

### Revealing the God of the Bible

*Dr. David Stoop, one of the executive editors of The Life Recovery Bible, spoke in a workshop held at the International Conference on Christian Counseling. He pointed out that there is a long period of time between the fall of humanity in the third chapter of Genesis and the healing from sin brought about by the death and resurrection of Jesus Christ in chapters 27 and 28 of the book of Matthew. The way Dr. Stoop put it, "God was hurt . . . all through the Old Testament."*

*Dr. Stoop stated, "The earlier the injury and the deeper the injury, the longer it is going to take to forgive." He then introduced a very interesting phrase, which you may want to remember in your own counseling experiences: Don't Push the River. What this little phrase means is, Don't try to rush the counseling process as the person moves toward healing. Sometimes pushing clients into quick forgiveness, either for themselves or others, may excuse sin rather than actually resulting in true forgiveness.*

How do we reveal the true character of God to our clients? First, by our own communication of love, respect, and dignity for the client, we help him or her to feel that God is a shelter for people to come to in the time of emergency or oppression: "You have been a shelter for me" (Ps. 61:3) and "The Lord also will be a refuge for the oppressed" (Ps. 9:9).

Second, the counselor helps the client understand that the Lord provides, in His personhood, a safe place for a person to live, without having to keep up a personal guard against invasion or knowledge of the truth about oneself: "Be my strong habitation" (Ps. 71:3). A person who begins to learn the personality of God begins to find a sense of peace and security, a place in which risk can be taken to build commitment, relationships, and communication with other people. Clients will not sense this "safe place" if they still believe God is against them or wants to punish them. Clients need to learn God's true attitude toward them because of the completed work of Jesus Christ on the cross. The counselor helps this process by introducing the client, through appropriate Scripture homework assignments, to what God Himself says about the client. One example is Jeremiah 29:11, "I know the plans I have for you . . . plans to prosper you and not to harm you, plans to give you a hope and a future" (NIV).

Third, as the counselor models the true nature of God, the client begins to find the strength to venture out and to do things that need to be done in life: "Be my rock of refuge" (Ps. 31:2).

Sometimes, within the counseling process, people are able to work through the things their overly rigid consciences or overly wounded emotions have projected onto the personality of God. They are able to find the strength they need, as they explore the personality of God in prayer and experience the truths of such Scriptures as Psalm 18:2; Psalm 27:5; Psalm 31:2; Psalm 61:2; and the marvelous promise of Isaiah 32:2, "The shadow of a great rock in a weary land."

The counselor models the character of God in the counseling relationship in order to allow the client to gradually shed false images of God. Through this modeling, the client begins to move from the relationship with the counselor to a true and emotionally enduring secure relationship with God the Father.

The counselor is not an attorney who tries to defend God against the accusations of the client. The counselor is one who comes alongside the client and helps to strengthen those parts of the client's perception and belief that parallel the truth about God as it is revealed in Scripture.

---

✋ **Skill Builder 8.4**  Add to your inventory of Scripture suitable for use in counseling. Look up the following Scriptures, which relate to the character and nature of Jesus Christ. Mark them in your Bible, or begin to index them on your computer for future reference. Write a one-word note about the character of Christ in the space provided.

JESUS WAS/IS . . .

Psalm 22:1 _____

Isaiah 53:7 _____

Isaiah 63:1 _____

Matthew 11:29 _____

Matthew 27:35 _____

Mark 3:35 _____

Luke 24:6 _____

1 Corinthians 1:30 _____

Ephesians 2:14 _____

Hebrews 2:17 _____

Hebrews 4:15 _____

Hebrews 13:6 _____

1 Peter 2:22 _____

1 Peter 2:23 _____

2 Peter 3:18 _____

---

## Working through Problems in Prayer

*A young preacher came to me with an unusual dilemma. He was opening a group home for addicted young men and needed a vehicle to transport them between the group home, the church, and their various social work and legal appointments. Since the young preacher was "living on faith" for himself and the needs of his family, he had no extra money with which to buy a vehicle. The question he asked me was whether or not he had the right to pray for God to give him a vehicle for this purpose. The Bible states in 1 Corinthians 12:9 that one of the "instant gifts" the Holy Spirit bestows on some occasions is the gift of faith. Although it is more common for me to have either the gifts of knowledge, wisdom, or discernment operate in counseling, I sometimes find God enables me to have this "gift of faith" to pray with people for certain situations.*

*In this case I felt strongly that God was in favor of this positive and unselfish purpose, and I encouraged the young preacher to pray, asking God to give him a vehicle. I even offered to pray with him toward that purpose. About a* *week later he said he had a new problem. He had received $1,000 for the purchase of a vehicle, but it had come from his father, with whom he did not feel "spiritually in tune". He wanted to know if it was righteous for him to accept this "tainted" money. He also seemed to feel God was being a little "cheap" about the whole thing, since he did not really think you could buy much of a car for $1,000!*

*This is a good example of where the enthusiasm of a counselor can backfire in the counseling process. My enthusiasm for his anticipated miracle almost shut me out of the painful conflicts he was experiencing, both in the area of his alienation from his father and in the area of his pride, where he wanted God to give him a brand new car rather than whatever he could buy for $1,000.*

*Therefore, the second session was not a session of motivation but one in which I needed to return to empathetic counseling, value sorting, and revealing scriptural principles. By the close of the session he had determined that God would want him to accept the money from his father as an affirmation of their relationship and a gesture of reconciliation. However, he was not completely sure God would provide him an adequate car for $1,000.*

*The following week when he came to see me he was rejoicing. He had found a Volkswagen minibus that a mechanic would sell him for $1,000, tax included! Additionally, when the man heard that he was a preacher and about the planned use of the van, he offered to put all new seats as well as a reconditioned engine in the vehicle.*

Many of my counseling students have experienced significant answers to prayer in their lives, which have increased their confidence in praying for miracles with their clients. Yet even those who believe in answers to prayer often find themselves in conflict regarding the answers they receive.

One student reported that when she was ten years old she prayed her father would stop abusing her mother. The prayer was answered, and the physical abuse stopped. However, the father was still subject to extreme mood swings (in her phrase, "chemical imbalance") from which he was not healed. Even when a miracle does take place, counseling issues often remain.

Some miracles may or may not be interpreted by the client as supernatural at the time. Another student told us about his mother: "She had a severe heart attack and died. The doctor revived her, but I believe it was God. I look back and realize it was a miracle of healing." The work of the counselor may be to help the client put a satisfactory evaluation on what has been experienced.

Prayer is not always positively answered. The disappointment of unfulfilled prayer may also be a focus for counseling, as in this teenaged girl's experience: "My youth leader was very sick. I remember praying with two friends for her healing. While we were praying, the phone rang. It was our church pastor, telling us that Sharon had just passed away." Without effective counseling, this type of "unanswered prayer" could destroy a person's faith.

In contrast, major escapes from disaster are often experienced as answers to prayer. Another student shared: "I was in a serious accident; we hit an 18-wheeler Sunoco gas truck head on. The station wagon was totaled. The driver and I walked out alive." She explained, "Prior to the accident, I knew we were going to hit. I quickly prayed to God for His protection. It was a miracle we got out alive!"

This student, without any specific counseling about her traumatic near-death incident, was able to integrate her overall positive belief in a God who saves, protects, and delivers from trouble. Other individuals may need counseling support to see the hand of God in such a situation.

**Skill Builder 8.5** Write out a counseling (not preaching) probe in response to each of the following "faith-or-foolishness" concerns.

EXAMPLE

*Client:* "Pastor, I'd like you to help me pray for a new Mustang convertible because I think they are really great cars!"

*Counseling Probe:* "Tell me a little bit about what you plan to do with this convertible if you get it."

PRACTICE

A. *Client:* "We have to move in six weeks, and I really want God to provide us a house with a good school district for the children, and one that is also close to my husband's job."

*Counseling Probe:* _____

_____

_____

**B.** *Client:* "I just would really like to take my paycheck this week and put it on the lottery, because I believe I really know what the winning numbers will be!"

*Counseling Probe:*_____

_____

## Prayer Disciplines for Counselors

> *In his devotional classic* The Practice of Prayer, *G. Campbell Morgan says that "the reason many people do not have their prayers answered is because they are unwilling to follow the instructions about prayer which Jesus gave when He taught the model prayer which we call The Lord's Prayer."*

The Bible directs us to pray for the sick (James 5:14-15), encourages us to believe for miracles (James 5:16-18), and reminds us to comfort those who hurt (2 Cor. 1:4). Often, however, we may feel inadequate to these spiritual counseling tasks because our own private prayer life has yet to experience the necessary development for us to become a prayer support to others.

Dr. Morgan points out that many people who say they believe in prayer are sporadic in its practice. He indicates that the most important verse in the Bible regarding this may be, "But you, when you pray, go into your room, and when you have shut your door, pray to your Father who is in the secret place; and your Father who sees in secret will reward you openly" (Matt. 6:6). Dr. Morgan indicates that the "but" at the beginning of this passage is in contrast to Jesus' comments about hypocrites who want to pray in public. They want

to be seen as spiritual by other people rather than wanting to pray in private so that the prayer might be genuinely directed to God.

One value of private prayer for us as counselors is in keeping our heart pliable before God, listening for God's response rather than parading our piety or treating God like a celestial servant. The motives of a counselor very often are more critical than their actions, although our actions, when appropriately investigated, may betray our motives!

**Skill Builder 8.6** Describe a positive experience you have had with private prayer.

_____

_____

_____

_____

_____

## Prayer Disciplines for Clients

_When I was a teenage cadet at The Salvation Army School for Officers in New York City, I had three roommates. The most interesting of these was a guy named Ed. When he decided to become spiritual, he took the Bible literally about going "into your closet to pray." He actually prayed in his closet every morning—right there with the old gym socks and sneakers! Privacy is hard to find in a four-man dorm room._

Dr. Morgan teaches, "Christ instructed His disciples that in the life of each one of them there must be a special place, a special time and a special method, whereby in quietness and loneliness, every third person being excluded, each one should pray."

When clients come to us with complaints that their prayers are not being answered, it is well for us to use some probes to investigate with them:

- How they pray
- When they pray
- The objects for which they pray
- The motives behind their requests

Although these may not sound like very spiritual probes, the counselor's systematic investigation helps the client determine the condition of his or her heart. This investigation may actually be a greater aid to the person's faith than the most positive injunctions the person hears from the pulpit.

While emphasizing the need for lonely, quiet times of prayer, in which there is no codependency on other people, Dr. Morgan also reminds his students of the Scripture that says, "If two of you agree on earth concerning anything that they ask, it will be done for them by My Father in heaven. For where two or three are gathered together in My name, I am there in the midst of them" (Matt. 18:20). Dr. Morgan teaches not only the need for the

discipline of lonely prayer without interpersonal overtones but also that there is a need for fellowship and support in prayer.

The counselor working with a client who is struggling with issues of prayer and faith would do well to inquire whether the client is more inclined toward private prayer, small-group prayer, or passively watching other people pray in a worship service. This investigation will be instructive in helping the counselor come alongside the client, in support of the development of the client's faith but in an informed way. Those areas of prayer that the client avoids are especially relevant since there may be symptoms of emotional wounds or spiritual immaturity that will later surface in the counseling process.

**Skill Builder 8.7** Describe what is psychologically and spiritually wrong with the following statement.

*Client:* "I don't think Marsha really meant to hurt me when she did all those awful things to me."

Problem Analysis: _____

_____

_____

Now write a short prayer for the people in each of the following situations to pray.

1. A person who is seeking to be forgiven for the sin of adultery: _____

_____

_____

2. A person who wants to forgive someone else who has financially cheated

him or her: _____

_____

_____

Using Jesus' model prayer in Matthew 6:6-18, note specific problems in the following prayer situations.

EXAMPLE

*Client:* "I am praying that the man who ran over my dog will get his own leg broken in some way! It hardly seems fair for my dog to get hurt and that man to get away without any problems at all!"

*Problem Analysis:* Lack of forgiveness
*Scripture:* Matthew 6:12

PRACTICE

A. *Client:* "God, please let that new blonde girl in the office be willing to go out with me, even though my divorce from Shirley is not yet final."

*Problem Analysis:* _____

_____

*Scripture:* _____

_____

B. *Client:* "I want everybody in this congregation to know I am praying earnestly for Joe's knee, which he broke skiing last week."

*Problem Analysis:* _____

_____

*Scripture:* _____

_____

C. *Client:* "I want God to make me rich and famous."

*Problem Analysis:* _____

_____

*Scripture:* _____

_____

## Sorting Out Prayers

Is God the author of miracles for our clients? He is, but many of our clients who pray for miracles miss their fulfillment because of their emotional wounds. Spiritual and personal immaturity may make it difficult for them to receive from God unless the divine answer comes in a very specific, sugar-coated fashion.

In your taped interview practice, you will often find that your role is not to be the one who "agrees in prayer" with the client. Many Christian clients have friends and pastors who can do that with them. The task of the counselor, operating in faith, is to help the person sort through exactly what is being prayed for, the why of it, and what the person is willing to receive if God is willing to give him or her a positive answer. If the job of the pastor is to help the person exercise his or her faith for a miracle, the job of the counselor is often to help the person sort through his or her emotions and concerns in order to accept the miracle in the way in which God delivers it!

The Skill Builders in this chapter and the resources that follow are designed to help you think about the ways in which prayer can become a vital component of spiritual counseling. Experiment with introducing prayer into your taped practice interview in a way that is meaningful for both you and your client.

Chapter Eight **BACK TALK**

Please answer the following questions for this chapter:

1. What is the main point of this chapter? _____

_____

_____

_____

2. What was your favorite illustration/story in this chapter? Why?_____

_____

_____

_____

3. Describe a personal experience you have had as a counselor or counselee

(formal or informal) that relates to the content of this chapter: _____

_____

_____

_____

4. What question(s) do you have after reading this chapter?_____

_____

_____

_____

5. What would you like to learn more about in this course?_____

_____

_____

_____

Chapter Eight **TAPED INTERVIEW ANALYSIS**

Name:_____

Date:_____

Interview Number:_____

1. What was the client's presenting (initial) problem or opportunity?_____

_____

_____

_____

2. What skills did you attempt to practice in this interview? Give one or more

examples: _____

_____

_____

_____

3. What do you feel you did best in this interview? _____

_____

_____

_____

_____

4. What do you feel you need to improve upon based on this interview? ___

_____

_____

_____

5. Describe any surprises, shifts in direction or content, or significant positive

or negative turning points in this interview: _____

_____

_____

_____

_____

6. How was the client thinking and/or feeling by the end of this interview? __

_____

_____

_____

_____

7. If this were an interview series, what do you think might happen in the next interview?_____

_____

_____

_____

_____

8. What did you learn most about the process of personal counseling from conducting this interview? _____

_____

_____

_____

_____

Chapter Eight **THE COUNSELOR'S LIBRARY**

Consider adding one or more of these books to your counseling library:

Clark, Glen. *I Will Lift Up Mine Eyes.* New York: Harper and Brothers, 1937.
> Mr. Clark, a Christian high-school track coach, spent a lifetime teaching effective, Scripture-based approaches to prayer. This book may be read as a whole or may be used as a daily course in prayer.

DeJong, Peter, and I. K. Berg. *Interviewing for Solutions.* Pacific Grove, Cal.: Brooks/Cole Publishers, 1998.
> This excellent clinical social-work text includes a section on helping clients define the miracles they are hoping for. A secular book written by Christian authors using Christian priciples.

Laubach, Frank C. *Prayer, The Mightiest Force in the World.* Westwood, N.J.: Flemming Revell Company, 1946.
> This inspiring book on prayer by missionary and literacy expert Frank Laubach has shown many how to develop an effective prayer life.

Ryan, Juanita, and Dale Ryan. *Recovery from Distorted Images of God.* Downers Grove, Ill.: InterVarsity Press, 1992.
> This highly effective fifty-nine-page Bible study, with journal questions included, has helped many to give up hating or running from a false and punitive God and to embrace the loving, caring God of the Bible. Other volumes in this series include *Recovery From Family Dysfunctions, Recovery From Shame, Recovery From Bitterness, Recovery From Abuse, Recovery From Loss, Recovery From Addictions,* and *Recovery from Codependency.*

*The Spirit Filled Life Bible.* Nashville: Thomas Nelson, 1991.
> Respected pastor Jack W. Hayford, Litt.D., is the general editor of this excellent study Bible, which has many helps in the areas of prayer and the spiritual authority of the believer.

Doc & Duck © 1999 Andrew J. Cheydleur

# Specialty Intervention Skills

*If a demon had come around the rational, decent Episcopalian household in which I was raised, it would have slunk away very disappointed. No one would have needed to exorcize it, because it simply would have been ignored. Demons did not exist in our world, because we did not believe they existed. It would have been very difficult for one who tried to invade that house. The frustrated demon would have found itself shunned and ignored, with no real attention being given to it. In one sense there is a great strength in being brought up in that kind of stable, rational background. However, it does tend to handicap one as a beginning counselor in dealing with some of the difficult issues of natural and supernatural evil that we all face.*

IN THE EARLY 1800s, people who acted in bizarre ways were often thought to be possessed by evil spirits. There was little thought of possible organic or emotional causes for their behavior. They were often locked up and sometimes beaten or killed.

In the early 1900s, people who acted in bizarre ways were often thought to be mentally ill. There was little thought of possible physical or demonic causes for their behavior. They were often locked up and sometimes beaten or given extreme electric shocks.

In the mid to late 1900s, people who acted in bizarre ways were often thought to have a chemical imbalance. There was less sympathy for emotional therapy and little thought of possible demonic causes for their behavior. They were often locked up for short periods and then given chemical straitjackets. They were locked up again if they "refused to take their meds."

How much has our world really changed? Most people would rather avoid the problems of others than learn how to intervene in a helping fashion.

In this chapter you will learn specific intervention steps for challenging evil. You will also be challenged to care for hurting people who do not have any demonic component in their woundedness.

In his strategic book *The People of the Lie,* psychiatrist M. Scott Peck shows that evil is far more pervasive than most of us who see ourselves as middle-class people would like to admit. (See the "The Counselor's Library" section at the end of the chapter for more information about this very important book.)

---

### ༃ Skill Builder 9.1

Have you ever experienced (either related to yourself or to another person) a spirit that you would label as demonic? If so, describe the circumstances, the evidence of or behavior of the evil spirit, and your or the other person's

response/reaction: _____

_____

_____

_____

_____

What do you feel about the possible interaction of emotional, physical, and demonic factors in human problems? _____

_____

_____

_____

_____

---

## Challenged by the Demonic

*While directing the Christian Psychiatric Clinic, we had an unusual instance of demonic involvement. In this instance, a very alienated young schizophrenic man came to the clinic wearing mirrored sunglasses. He would not take them off for the receptionist or the therapist, who was a licensed clinical social worker. He only took them off at night when he was alone. After six or eight weeks of therapy, a therapeutic alliance was established and some progress was made, but the therapist felt he had reached a plateau and could go no further with the therapy.*

*Tim's sunglasses fetish had begun during a period in which he had some "casual" occult involvement.*

*As a Christian, the therapist had spiritual authority to deal with the demonic activity himself, but since he had limited experience in this area, he requested we bring in a counseling pastor from a church who was familiar with demonic activity and also was experienced in mental health team interventions. With the permission of the client, the counseling pastor came the following week and said a very simple, nondramatic prayer of deliverance. After that, the man was able to take off his sunglasses and greet our receptionist with some degree of openness and began to move considerably forward in the therapeutic process.*

Dealing with presumed or possible demonic influence in a structured setting like a Christian counseling clinic is a very disciplined process. But what do you do if you encounter an evil influence in a less-structured environment?

*One sunny Sunday morning, my rational middle-class worldview was abruptly challenged. I was teaching an adult elective Sunday school class in counseling skills for lay counselors at a large metropolitan church when a short, rough-looking, bull-necked older man pushed his way to the front and abruptly sat down.*

*Halfway through my lecture on "Accurate Empathy," he impatiently interrupted and asked, "What do you do if you have a demon?"*

*Not missing a beat and modeling my own best reflective style, I responded, "So your question is what a person should do who has a demon."*

*The man answered, "Yes; I have a demon in me who is telling me to murder someone!"*

What was going on here? Did this man truly have a demon? Was this a homicidal person who needed to be reported to the police? Or was this simply a distraught soul who had found a way to seek attention from church groups?

๚๛ **Skill Builder 9.2** Write a probe or prompt in your response to the following statements.

EXAMPLE

*Client:* "Pastor, I think I have a demon inside me."
*Probe/Prompt:* "Could you tell me a little bit more about what makes you think you have a demon?"

PRACTICE

A. *Client:* "I have an evil voice inside telling me things I should do to hurt people, and I really don't want to do these things. Pastor, what should I do?"

*Probe/Prompt:* _____

_____

_____

B. *Client:* "I think the reason I am getting so fat is I have a hot-fudge-sundae demon. What do you think?"

*Probe/Prompt:* _____

_____

_____

Write a paragraph describing what you might be feeling or thinking if you encountered the clients who are quoted in A and B.

EXAMPLE

*Does he really believe this, or is it just a figure of speech?*

PRACTICE

A. _____

_____

B. _____

_____

## Provisional Acceptance of Client Self-Statements

*I said to the man, "Do you really believe you have a demon inside you who wants you to commit a murder?" The man answered in the affirmative.*

*I had recently attended a workshop conducted by Pastor Ed Piorek of the Vineyard Christian Fellowship, who outlined some key issues for counselors encountering various aspects of demonic activity. I remembered that the first issue is simply gaining control of the particular situation we face. Then, drawing on my psychology training, I wanted to form an "index of lethality" in my mind regarding this man's danger to the public or to himself.*

*I asked him if he had a specific person in mind, and he replied that he did but that he did not have a plan in mind at this point. (The man did not tell me his name or the name of his target, or I might have been under legal obligation to report the potential harm to the police and/or to the potential victim. Various state laws differ on this point.)*

*Whether this was simply a disruptive individual or one who really had a disruptive and murderous spirit, it was important that he not control the rest of the class. So, using the empathy-sandwich technique outlined earlier in this book, I set up an "appointment" for him to come back to the Sunday school class the following week for the demon to be exorcized. The man immediately left the room.*

Several years earlier, I would have been inclined not to take seriously the man's self-statement of demonization. However, I had witnessed enough situations over the past few years that I was not going to tell him that what he told me was not an accurate assessment of his own situation. At the same time, I refused to let the angry or demonized man set the agenda for the class.

Pastor Piorek suggests that an interview is usually valuable to enhance diagnosis and discernment and to develop a course of action. One of his key points is that deliverance prayer is a part of some greater healing process. Demonic activity does not usually happen in the absence of emotional wounding or other predisposing causes that allow the demon to get hold of the person. In this case it was clear the man who had come into our class had extreme anger and bitterness against the other person, whom he considered to have severely wronged him. While a secular psychologist might have dismissed the "I-have-a-demon" statement as a colorful figure of speech, the anger was quite real and could certainly allow for some sort of demonic attachment.

**Skill Builder 9.3** Suggest some of the broader areas of emotional healing that may be connected with the following statements about demonic activity.

EXAMPLE

*Client:* "I have a voice inside telling me to kill myself. Sometimes it gets so loud, I just can't stand it!"

*Possible Healing Issues:* Suicidal ideation, depression, unacknowledged anger, alienation

PRACTICE

A. *Client:* "The devil will not let me go to school. He says he will hurt me in some way if I go there."

*Possible Healing Issues:* _____

_____

_____

B. *Client:* "Pastor, I believe my sister has a secret demon in her."

*Possible Healing Issues:* _____

_____

_____

## A Seventeen-Step Process

> *The next Sunday all was in readiness. The adult Sunday school class members, many of whom were deeply committed Christian people, had been praying during the week. I asked for personal prayer from some of the supportive people in my own life. The visiting pastor from the inner city attended with his wealth of experience.*

In his workshop Ed Piorek recommended a seventeen-step process for removing a demon from a suffering person's life. He had stated that "crowding a spirit out is usually much easier than shouting one out" (step 1). He recommended a person first be invited to receive salvation and forgiveness through Jesus Christ and then ask to be filled with the Holy Spirit. The next step would be to shut out any access points for the demons through inviting the person to personal repentance and renouncing all demonic involvement (step 2). It is very important that the client actively participate in this process (step 3) rather than passively expecting the counselor to do some sort of "magic trick" to make him or her feel better.

Pastor Piorek also helpfully recommended using prayer teams (step 4) if they are formed of people who have experience in this area and are not simply curiosity seekers.

> *I asked the Sunday school class not to publicize this event, so we would not have curiosity seekers the following Sunday. During the week, I contacted an experienced rescue-mission pastor from inner-city Los Angeles, who regularly worked with mentally ill and demon-possessed people in the most difficult part of the city.*

It is important to point out that "mentally ill" and "demon possessed" are not the same category, although some of the symptoms may mimic each other.

> *A few minutes after the beginning of the session, the short, rough-looking, bull-necked older man stomped his way into our classroom.*

It is good to note that it is common for demons to want to interrupt things and draw attention to themselves. Therefore, in many situations, it is better to deal with a demonic issue within the privacy of a prayer room, pastoral study, or office, rather than allowing the demonic manifestations to have an audience. Here, the class was made up of mature Christians who could be supportive to the deliverance process.

> *Our visiting pastor asked the man to sit in a chair and treated the man with love and dignity (step 5). He had discussed with me in advance what he was going to do and observed that maintaining eye contact (step 6) is often critical. In contradiction to some public deliverance ministries, he emphasized firmness as more important than loudness (step 7) in commanding a demonic spirit to leave a person. (For some biblical examples of this process, see Mark 1:21-26; 5:1-20; 9:17-29.)*

> *Our visiting minister did not ask the spirit to identify itself by name. He did, however, ask the man whether he would mind if some of the men in the class held on to his shoulders from behind while he was sitting in the chair (step 8). The man very meekly and*

*passively indicated that this would be acceptable to him. They held on to his feet in front before he prayed for the spirit to come out.*

*However, when the visiting minister commanded the spirit to come out (step 9), it was as though a lightning bolt had struck the room! The man began to thrash and twist, and it took all four men who were holding on to him to keep him in the chair. He was squirming sideways and seemed to be ready to fall out of the chair or roll onto the floor at any minute!*

*Ten members of the Sunday school class quietly prayed while all this activity was going on (step 10). The visiting minister continued to pray, rebuking the spirit (step 11) and telling it to stop bothering the man (step 12). He told the spirit to be quiet (step 13) and to come out and not enter the man again (step 14). After what seemed like a long time (but probably was only three or four minutes), the man quieted down, his facial muscles relaxed, and his arms and legs untensed as he slumped in his chair as though he were waking up from a long nap.*

*We asked him how he felt, and he replied that he felt all right but tired. I interviewed him (step 15) concerning his homicidal intentions, and he said that the evil spirit had left him and that he had no desire to murder anyone.*

In individual counseling, such a deliverance episode would be followed up by continued counseling (step 16) and additional prayer (step 17).

The pastoral counselor should also anticipate other problems, whether emotional or supernatural, that might begin to surface following such a tremendous and unusual crisis experience. However, I never did find out the name of our class visitor, and he never attended again. I anxiously watched the metropolitan papers for several weeks with some fear that our intervention might not have been successful, but did not find any mention in the paper of a violent murder that could have been in any way related to this person.

---

**Skill Builder 9.4** Using your Bible as a reference, look up several examples where Jesus or others effectively cast a demon or demons out of someone or broke their hold over someone. Also review Matthew 10:1; Mark 1:21-27; Luke 11:14-28; John 6:28-29; Acts 4:29; 5:16. Then write your own brief statement of Christian authority over these evil spirits, which you could use as the basis of a deliverance prayer if you were called upon to do so sometime in the future.

Scripture References You Reviewed: _____

_____

_____

_____

Statement of Your Christian Authority: _____

_____

_____

_____

_____

## Exercising Caution with Children

*My wife and I visited a church that was known for its prayer ministry. That Sunday morning, a young couple brought their restless and crying two-year-old to the front and whacked him on the seat a number of times while shouting for the demon to come out of him. The lady pastor looked horrified but did not intervene.*

Be very cautious about diagnosing an evil spirit in a very young child in real life (unlike the movies). Issues of physical development, such as gaps in the myelin sheath that insulates the nerves in the spinal column, and parenting issues, etc., should be thoroughly reviewed before any demonic assumption is made.

Also, many children are brought to pastors by parents who think they "have a demon" due to behavior problems, when the children are simply hyperactive and may respond to appropriate medication. Some children exhibit emotional stress due to undetected child abuse. Most children with severe problems should receive a physical examination prior to any other spiritual or mental-health diagnosis.

**Skill Builder 9.5** How would you respond to a young mother who came to you with this question?

*Client:* "My son is a mentally challenged little boy, and I know he does some disruptive actions when he knows better. Some things he does are pretty destructive, and I sometimes wonder if he has an evil spirit."

*Counselor:* _____

_____

_____

_____

_____

## Using Spiritual Authority with Care

*A young Christian woman sent me the following letter:*

> *My brother is apparently involved in a satanic cult. He is a high priest and
> sent me some pictures of himself wearing an upside-down cross. I immedi-
> ately prayed and tore the pictures up because I felt an incredible evil sense
> while seeing them.*

All of our listening and challenging skills cannot provide the full healing or
therapy we seek to give. This complex and sensitive listening is the preparation and follow-up for our sensitive and wise use of the spiritual authority
*(Exousia)* God has delegated to us and through which His inherent power
*(Dunamis)* flows.

> *This woman went on to state she was afraid she would be harmed as an adult
> by her brother in a way similar to how he had harmed her as a child.*

At the very least, caution and self-protection would seem to be indicated
for her in this situation. Remember, she—not the evil brother—would be
your client if she came to you. The "rule of thumb" is that the only client
you have is the person you have in front of you, not the person he or she is
talking about.

When we learn the best techniques but somehow fail to include the
power of God, we, and our clients, lose a great deal. Leanne Payne puts it
this way in her deeply insightful book *The Healing Presence:*

> *The greater peril today, however, lies in the Christian's loss of his own superior
> truth system, both intellectual and symbolic. With this truth he is to evaluate
> the systems and therapies of the day. If he is to move in God's power and
> authority, the servant of the Lord must know that even the best wisdom of the
> day is insufficient and cannot fully grasp the mystery of the human spirit, soul,
> and body. Looking to God and listening to Him is essential.*

A senior pastor whose church has a number of members who have been
subjected to occult experiences reminds his prayer counselors:

> *One of the cautions in using deliverance prayer, even for adults, is that an
> overly extreme mysticism can become a hindrance to the process. It's important
> to know not only the power but the limitations of these spirits of evil intent.*
> *For instance, demons can speak through the person who is bound and ques-*

*tion the right of authority of the deliverance minister; i.e., "If you have sin in your life, you have no power over me." This is evil deception and should not be paid any attention. Your authority over demons is not based on your own righteousness but on the "blood of the Lamb" (Rev. 12:11).*

*Or similarly, "I have a right to be here because this person wants me to be here or did some mischievous deed allowing me to be here."*

*All demonic statements such as these should be treated as gossip from a liar.*

Note: As a Christian counselor, you are acting on the authority of Christ (Luke 10:17; Mark 16:17), not on your own authority or that of the victim.

It is sometimes helpful for the client's family to be involved in the deliverance process and be taught how to take prayer authority in the case of future problems in this area in order to avoid long-term dependence on you as a counselor.

If you come from a background that has little encounter with demonic phenomena, you may find it helpful to read Kevin Springer's insightful book *Power Encounters.* Spiritual counselors for whom these are new experiences should also remember not to become fixated on a particular episode or report. Instead, move back into an empathy role with the client to facilitate the client's processing of that experience before moving on to practical action planning about nonsupernatural events.

Roger Bufford's more clinical work *Counseling and the Demonic* will help you attain a cautious confidence for this difficult—but important—area of counseling ministry. It is volume 17 in the thirty-four-volume Resources for Counseling series, edited by Dr. Gary Collins.

**Skill Builder 9.6** How would you respond to the young Christian woman who sent the letter?

1. Does she have an obligation to talk to her brother? Why or why not? ___
_____
_____

2. Should she stay away from him? Why or why not? _____
_____
_____

3. What would you say to her? _____
_____
_____

Look up the following Scripture references regarding "delegated authority," and copy the Bible verses as you find them.

1. Matthew 9:6 _____
_____

2. Matthew 10:1 _____
_____

3. Luke 10:19 _____
_____

Now write one paragraph to describe your own feelings about having authority delegated to you from God the Father to be a healer of other people.

_____
_____
_____
_____
_____

## Where There Is No Demon

*Sandra did not come to us as a client but as a custodian. She was a big, raw-boned young woman who had grown up on a farm. She turned out to be capable at electrical and plumbing repair, had excellent cleaning skills, and refused help from anyone on the staff when large packages were delivered or drums of cleaning supplies needed to be moved around the building. Much to the chagrin of some of our more traditional female staff members, Sandra was adamant about being self-sufficient in her job.*

*As we got to know Sandra, we learned although she was not a lesbian, she was not very happy about being a woman. Her last job had been as a secretary in an insurance company where she had had to wear a skirt and hosiery every day. She simply hated being closed in and forced to dress in what she considered to be awkward clothes.*

*We also learned Sandra had some history of depression and suicidal ideation, as well as a history of alcohol abuse (if not actual addiction), so we suggested she see a therapist at another clinic. To avoid any conflict of interest with her job, it was recommended she join Alcoholics Anonymous, and she did. These two supportive relationships, along with the self-esteem she was developing in a job that did not require her to conform to any traditional role, resulted a year later in her coming to the staff Christmas party wearing an attractive dress! Of course, we did not make a fuss over her dressy appearance, since her regular job really was more appropriately done in jeans and a sweatshirt. We were, however, pleased to see the progress in her own self-esteem as indicated in her appearance at the Christmas party.*

*Sandra's farm-life background as a child was far from ideal. She had been beaten and abused and caused to think she was no good as a person and especially undesirable as a little girl. She had learned a shame-based approach to life that had inhibited her from discovering her own natural talents or accepting anything about herself as being good.*

It is important to remember that many (perhaps most) human problems have no demonic component at all and are instead tied to deep emotional wounds. Even where demonic activity may be present, emotional trauma may be present as well.

When a client comes to us whose primary life stance is "I am no good," that psychological posture is going to permeate every aspect of the counseling relationship. Normal compliments from the counselor will be seen as either invasive or dishonest. Advice from friends or support groups may either be loudly exaggerated or angrily rejected.

It is particularly important for counselors who are working with clients who are having supernatural experiences, whether demonic or miraculous, to become and maintain themselves as the calm, stable resource that is predictable and dependable. A client's emotions may escalate in a very short period of time. Unfortunately, many of the people in such a client's life will thrive on the roles of advice giver, power broker, and manipulator. The counselor must be particularly guarded in avoiding any kind of manipulative role, as well as many kinds of directive roles. All guidance must be very carefully selected to support the client's "baby steps" toward a world of sanity, stability, and self-acceptance.

> *In conducting a program review at one of The Salvation Army Adult Rehabilitation Centers, I listened to the story of a young man who had graduated from the center a year before and returned to share with the current residents in the program. He said he had grown up in the slums of Philadelphia and had no expectations of any possible positive or stable life as a child, being shunted back and forth between relatives without any predictability or security. As a young adult, he had supported himself by mugging people in the Philadelphia subway in the early hours of the morning. (He had rationalized that he at least had the integrity not to mug people who were traveling in the daytime!)*
>
> *As a cocaine addict, he had needed a great deal of money to sustain his habit and had had no hope there was any life for him other than that of crime and addiction. At various time several relatives had tried to get him into rehabilitation programs, but because he had felt so hopeless about life, he had exited some of them and failed at others.*
>
> *Someone had referred him to this particular Salvation Army Center. He came at a time when he was particularly discouraged and somewhat frightened of increased police activity within the subway system. At the center he became involved with Narcotics Anonymous and accepted Jesus Christ as his Savior. During the telling of his story, he indicated that he had been living in a small Pennsylvania community for a year, had a job, and was consistently paying the rent for his own apartment. For some, this simple, undistinguished lifestyle might not seem to be miraculous, but for the man telling the story, his view was, "I had never believed it possible I would live a normal life!"*

The client who feels that "I don't deserve anything better" is often so traumatized by life that outpatient counseling will not work the necessary "magic" of transforming the person's attitudes toward him- or herself. Some type of long-term, residential setting, such as that represented by The Salvation Army Adult Rehabilitation Center, Teen Challenge, or a Christian inpatient therapy unit, may be necessary. This allows the person to have the adequate behavioral, emotional, and spiritual immersion that is necessary for him or her to reframe his or her attitudes toward him- or herself and God. Then he or she can move toward the possibility of a pleasant and positive future.

It is therefore important for each of us as counselors to acknowledge both the abilities and wounds we bring to the process of counseling as well as the limits of the settings in which we work. It is also important that we have developed appropriate referral sources for persons with specialized problems that we cannot effectively address.

---

**Skill Builder 9.7** Briefly list three things that have impacted positively on your self-esteem or emotional or spiritual health, either as a child, a teenager, or an adult.

1. _____

_____

2. _____

_____

3. _____

_____

Briefly list two things that have negatively impacted on your self-esteem or emotional or spiritual health, either during your childhood, teenage years, or as an adult.

1. _____

_____

2. _____

_____

Now list three things have negatively impacted on the self-esteem or emotional or spiritual health of people you have counseled.

1. _____

_____

2. _____

_____

3. _____

_____

## Accepting Ourselves As Healers

*"Who, me, a healer?" is what I would have said if anyone had given me that label as I stepped forward to receive my master's degree in the ceremony at Loyola University of Chicago. Yes, I had learned some counseling skills and experienced some successes in my internship, but I certainly would not have used that label. I thought it was too prideful, arrogant, because I did not come from a tradition that uses this sort of language.*

The role we have as counselors includes the role of being God's healing agents. There are two primary Greek words for *power* in the New Testament. The first is *dunamis,* which appears sixty-one times and usually means the inherent power that resides in God. The second word, *exousia,* is used sixty-seven times and means delegated legal authority, the power God delegates to us and uses through us to help and heal other people. Examples of *dunamis* are found in Luke 1:35; Matthew 6:13; Mark 5:30; and Acts 1:8. Examples of *exousia* are found in Matthew 9:6; Matthew 10:1; Luke 10:19.

Therefore, our authority to pray for others—for their spiritual, emotional, and physical healing—is based on the Word of God, the standard for all faith and practice for Christian persons.

Furthermore, our authority does not come from our strength or our righteousness but is based on the finished work of Christ, whose pure life, atoning death, and victorious resurrection show He has the power, authority, and desire to right every kind of wrong and heal every kind of disease.

Also, our power to act as healing agents is based on our developing the progressive disciplines of prayer. These include our worship of the Creator (not of ourselves, the created), our commitment to personal, up-to-date repentance, and an awareness that we have an advocate with the Father, to whom we continually refer in our private prayer.

Further, we base our role as counselors and healers on the role models of our faith. Of course, there are many biblical role models, such as Elijah, an ordinary man but one who prayed and saw answers to his prayers. We also look at historical role models such as evangelist D. L. Moody and missionary literacy expert Frank Laubach, who translated their lives of prayer into lives of positive life-changing action for other people. We also have contemporary role models that we have met in our own life, those to whom we look during times of need for reassurance and the possibility of serving as God's agents in a mixed-up and unpredictable world.

Each role model strengthens our awareness of the connection between purity and power, as outlined in the book of Hebrews and the three Epistles of John.

---

**Skill Builder 9.8**  List five things you think you could do to improve your effectiveness as a healing agent for other people.

1. One spiritual thing I could do is: _____

_____

2. One academic thing I could do is: _____

_____

3. One relational thing I could do is: _____

_____

4. One biblical thing I could do is: _____

_____

5. One self-developmental thing I could do is: _____

_____

---

## Healing within Counseling

You may come out of a religious culture with great emphasis on the dramatic and need to learn how to sort the real from the exaggerated. You may come from an emotionally and intellectually conservative background and need to learn to see the positive strength of miracles and admit the compulsive nature of actual evil. We each need to acknowledge and experience our spiritual gifts of wisdom, knowledge, discernment, and faith so that we can be used by God as effective healers within the counseling process. People are not simply healed on the surface but are deeply healed for a lifetime.

This chapter's Skill Builders and the books in The Counselor's Library will help you to explore your own unique, individual approach to the healing ministry.

After you have completed the Skill Builders, prepare to tape your last counseling training interview. Do not try to force this interview into any preconceived pattern or attempt to make it fit themes regarding demons, miracles, healing, etc. Just allow the interview to flow naturally, drawing on all the things you have learned in your previous training.

After you have completed this interview, listen to the tape, and make notes for yourself regarding any areas in which the supernatural might be relevant to the cognitive and emotional issues discussed.

Chapter Nine **BACK TALK**

Please answer the following questions for this chapter:

1. What is the main point of this chapter? _____
_____
_____
_____

2. What was your favorite illustration/story in this chapter? Why?_____
_____
_____

3. Describe a personal experience you have had as a counselor or counselee (formal or informal) that relates to the content of this chapter: _____
_____
_____

4. What question(s) do you have after reading this chapter?_____
_____
_____

5. What would you like to learn more about in this course?_____
_____
_____

Name:_____

Date:_____

Interview Number:_____

1. What was the client's presenting (initial) problem or opportunity?_____

_____

_____

_____

2. What skills did you attempt to pracice in this interview? Give one or more

examples: _____

_____

_____

3. What do you feel you did best in this interview? _____

_____

_____

_____

4. What do you feel you need to improve upon based on this interview? ____

_____

_____

5. Describe any surprises, shifts in direction or content, or significant positive

or negative turning points in this interview: _____

_____

_____

6. How was the client thinking and/or feeling by the end of this interview? ___

_____

_____

_____

7. If this were an interview series, what do you think might happen in the next interview? _____

_____

_____

8. What did you learn most about the process of personal counseling from conducting this interview? _____

_____

_____

Chapter Nine **THE COUNSELOR'S LIBRARY**

Consider adding one or more of these books to your counseling library:

Bufford, Roger K. *Counseling and the Demonic.* Resources for Counseling, vol. 17. Waco, Texas: Word, 1989.
> This is one of the very few books written about dealing with the demonic from a professional perspective. It is a valuable resource, as are all of the books in this series of specialty counseling topics, edited by Dr. Gary Collins.

Peck, M. Scott. *The People of the Lie: The Hope for Healing Human Evil.* New York: Simon and Schuster, 1983.
> Christian psychiatrist Dr. M. Scott Peck introduces us to encounters with evil in everyday life, from parents' crimes against their children to the Mylai massacre, and recommends a methodology of love.

Prince, Derek. *They Shall Expel Demons.* Grand Rapids: Chosen Books/Baker Book House, 1998.
> Derek Prince grew up in India, was educated at Oxford, and later became a pastor. His comprehensive book on deliverance is based on more than forty years of worldwide experience.

Springer, Kevin. *Power Encounters among Christians in the Western World.* San Franciso: Harper and Row, 1988.
> Mr. Springer's cosmology indicates the defeat of evil by good is always the result of a spiritual battle, not only in ancient times or missionary countries but here and now, beneath the rational facade of our Westernized culture. A number of Christian leaders are included.

Stoop, David, and Stephen Arterburn, eds. *The Life Recovery Bible,* New Living Translation. Wheaton, Ill.: Tyndale House, 1998.
> This marvelous work, available in hardcover or beautifully bound paperback, features intensive recovery and life-problem-resolution commentary by noted Christian psychologist Dr. David Stoop. Biographical sketches of Bible characters throughout include characters' strengths and accomplishments, weaknesses and mistakes, lessons from their lives, and key Scripture verses.

# PART FOUR

# CONTINUING EDUCATION

# Written Case Notes

As YOU BEGIN to do counseling with a number of people, you will eventually want to keep some notes so that you can keep track of what you did, and where you are going, for each person you are counseling.

## Value of Case Recording

While some counselors do not keep written notes of their interviews, most find it helpful to do so. As in the complex "SOAP" notes example below, careful case recording can help the counselor to keep track of and sort out the variety of issues that may arise in the counseling process.

In addition, good case notes allow the committed counselor to review past successes (and failures) as an ongoing means of self-supervision and professional development.

These notes become the record (or "case") of your counseling activities. There are a number of good systems for case recording, but two of those which are recommended for short-term counseling are called "DAP" and "SOAP."

## Basic "DAP" Case Notes

In the "DAP" system, there are three elements that are written down for each interview: D, for data; A, for assessment; and P, for plan:

**D—Data** In this system, the "D" part of your notes records the information you have collected for this interview. The data may include only information directly supplied by the person being counseled or may also include information supplied by other sources (family members, police, pastor, hospitals, etc.). This material is first recorded under "D" in summary form without evaluation as to its importance, truth, value, etc.

**A—Assessment** The "A" part of your notes follows the "D" part. This is your assessment of the information contained in the data section. This is the place where your opinion about the truth or the value of certain information is recorded. Some pastoral counselors also use this section to record their hunches, insights, and promptings from the Holy Spirit regarding what should be done with this person.

**P—Plan** After you have recorded your data and your assessment of it, you will want to record your plan. The plan is the agreement you and the person being counseled have made concerning what should be done (by either or both of you) between now and the next session. This plan is then reviewed at the beginning of the next session in order to provide accountability for both the counselor and the client.

Case notes do not always have to be complex. In many situations, clear and simple notes are all that is needed, as in the example below:

*(First Interview)*
*D. (data)*
*Mrs. Paula Smith is a thirty-two-year-old white mother of three, who comes to church services once or twice a month; she called for an appointment and came on Wednesday, July 12, 20__, to talk about her husband, Fred. She is afraid he is having an affair with someone at work, which is causing him to come home late several nights a week. He is moody and irritable toward the children; he also seems to have stopped having any sexual interest in Paula.*

*A. (assessment)*
*Mrs. Smith seems very nervous and fearful about life in general, not just about her husband. It sounds like she would rather not be home taking care of children and resents her husband's career. He may or may not be having an affair, but she hasn't talked to him about it. They do not communicate very well with each other.*

**P. (plan)**

*I asked Mrs. Smith to invite her husband to come with her to see me next Tuesday at 7:00 P.M. She seems sure he will come, and she said she will get a baby-sitter. I also asked her to read Ephesians chapter 5 during the week, and she said she would.*

## Complex "SOAP" Notes

The SOAP system is similar to the DAP system, but here the "D" or data section is expanded into two sections: "S," self-report, and "O," information supplied by others. Some pastoral counselors prefer the SOAP system because it allows them to be more clear in keeping track of the sources of information in their case notes. The "A," assessment, and "P," plan, sections are used in the same way as they are in the DAP system.

For a person with a number of distinct counseling concerns, such as (a) drug abuse, (b) family relationship, and (c) completion of education, some counselors separate the SOAP system into specific S-O-A-P notes for each distinct area of problem or potential discussed in the interview.

Sometimes a counseling situation contains several elements, and the case notes help the counselor to keep them straight, as in this example, in which numbers 1–5 are assigned to various aspects of this case in order to keep track of the various people and issues involved.

*(Fourth Interview)*

**S. (self-report)**

*S1—premarital counseling*  Joe states very strongly that he wants to marry Susan now, or as soon as possible. These premarital counseling sessions are of very little value, except to slow down the process. Susan states she is very much in love with Joe but wants to have the approval of her pastor and her parents before getting married. (They suggested the need for premarital counseling and referred her to me.)

*S2—housing*  Joe states he is starting to save money for a deposit on an apartment (as we suggested in interview #2) so he and Susan will not have to move into his room at his parents' house when they are married. So far he has saved $53.00.

*S3—education*  Last week Joe went to the high school to register for the evening GED program, which is one thing Susan said she would like him to finish before they get married. He says that he really doesn't need this for himself since he already has a job he likes, but he is willing to do anything for Susan.

*S4—pastor, journal, emotions*  Susan has not yet started keeping a journal of her feelings about this intended marriage, which she told the counselor that the pastor had suggested she do.

*S5—Susan's family and friends*  Also, Susan still has not introduced Joe to any of her friends at work (she is a teacher's aide), although she agreed to do this two weeks ago.

### O. (other-report)

*O1—Susan's family*  Susan's mother called me four times last week, wanting to know if I had persuaded Susan to "drop that oaf".

*O2—Susan's pastor*  Her pastor also called to say that her normally faithful church attendance has dropped off. He did not pry into the content of the counseling sessions.

*O3—Joe's family*  Joe's father called to "get the date" when the premarital counseling sessions would be completed so he could "rent the hall" for the wedding. He seems pleased about the wedding.

### A. (assessment)

Although Susan is seven years older than Joe, she has done very little dating and seems much less emotionally mature and independent. It almost seems like she wants me to make the decision about marriage for her. Joe is clear and concrete about his current goals, but they are very limited. He may try to push Susan into eloping in order to get away from all this "adult pressure" to slow down and complete personal goals first. Also, he seems afraid of losing Susan if too much time passes. This marriage could work, but it will need a great deal of outside emotional support from family and church and may need some financial support as well.

### P. (plan)

Joe and Susan have made new commitments to each of the plans already agreed to:

P1—Obtain the blessing of Sue's pastor (both)

P2—Obtain the blessing of Sue's parents (both)

P3—Save money for deposit, first and last month's rent for an apartment (Joe)

P4—Complete GED high school diploma (Joe)

P5—Start a journal of feelings and continue it for at least two weeks (Susan)

P6—Introduce Joe to her friends at work (Susan)

P7—Complete at least seven sessions of premarital counseling (both)

In addition to the above, I suggested a family group session be held with both sets of parents present. Joe and Susan will let me know next week if they are willing to do this.

## Additional Issues

As you see in the above examples, written case recording can range from practical and simple to elaborately complex. Most formal counseling agencies have a standard format that staff are expected to use.

All written records should be kept in a locked, safe place, and should not be transported. Written records should not be released to anyone other than the client or someone who has a signed written release from the client, unless there is a *valid* court order.

# Scripture-Based Values

AS A SPIRITUAL COUNSELOR, over a period of years you will come to develop a sense of the most common problems, issues, and value conflicts people present to you in your ministry. In dealing with these issues, you will also develop an awareness of specific Scriptures. Select those you are comfortable using and that have been proven over time to be effective in releasing your clients from bondage, clearing their minds, and propelling them into appropriate decisions and action steps. In order to start identifying scriptural values, competing values, and value conflicts, review the following biblical texts. The topics are those which Christian counselors often face with their clients. The areas considered are: ethics and business issues, social issues, sexual and relationship issues, expectancy and gratitude issues, and spiritual and emotional issues.

## Ethics and Business Issues

• A person with a scriptural value orientation exercises faithful accountability to God for people, resources, and material (Gen. 1:27-28; Matt. 25:14-23). A person with possible cultural or personal value conflicts in this area may be negligent, greedy, and/or exploitive of people, resources, or materials (Prov. 26:13-16; Matt. 25:24-30).

• A person with a scriptural value set accepts responsibility to exercise personal authority, as delegated by God, to improve his or her world (Prov. 29:2; John 14:12-14). A person with possible cultural or personal value conflicts in this area often avoids accountability for his or her own use of power but may criticize others in authority over him or her (Prov. 73:7-9; Matt. 7:1-5).

• An individual with a scriptural value orientation holds him- or herself accountable to God for integrity in business dealings and family life (Ps. 73:23-24; Rom. 12:17). On the other hand, an individual with possible cultural or personal value conflicts may deny responsibility before God for his or her lack of honesty in business and personal relationships (Job 24:13-17; Ezek. 22:27).

## Social Issues

• An individual with biblical values in this area uses skills, position, and strength to protect widows and children, particularly in church and family (Ps. 12:5, James 1:27). In contrast, a person with possible cultural or personal value conflicts in this area may be reluctant to be concerned for anyone other than him- or herself and his or her own success (Exod. 20:17; Matt. 25:41-45).

• An individual with a scriptural value base provides hospitality to strangers without neglecting his or her own family (Isa. 58:6-8; Matt. 25:34-36). An individual with possible cultural or personal value conflicts in this area may isolate him- or herself from those who are new, strange or different and, in the extreme, may even isolate him- or herself from his or her own family (Ps. 146:7-9; 1 John 2:10-11).

## Sexual and Relational Issues

• A man with scriptural values in this area sees women as individuals created by God and holds them in high esteem (Gen. 2:18; 2 Cor. 6:18). In contrast, a man with possible cultural or personal value conflicts in this area may oppress women or view them as disposable objects (Zech. 7:10; 1 Tim. 5:2).

• A single person with solid biblical values in this area respects his or her own body and the body of another single person as being held in trust for their future spouses (Deut. 22:13-19; Matt. 5:32). However, a single person with possible cultural and/or personal value conflicts in this area may fantasize about the personalities and/or about the bodies of other singles as if they were his or her personal property or opportunity, without regard to either his or her own future spouse or the future spouse of the object of his or her fantasies (2 Sam. 13:2, 14-16, 22; Matt. 15:18-19).

• A person exercising biblical values refuses to behave romantically toward anyone already married to someone else (Gen. 39:7-9; Matt. 19:5-6). A person with possible cultural or personal value conflicts in this area may feel that he or she can act toward someone who is married to another individual as if the two of them were not married (Exod. 20:14; Luke 16:18).

• A single believer exercising biblical values does not behave romantically toward nonbelievers (Exod. 34:14-17; Neh. 13:26-27). Unfortunately, a believer who has possible cultural or personal value conflicts in this area may feel that he or she has the freedom to behave romantically toward a nonbeliever (Deut. 7:3; 2 Cor. 6:14).

• A married man or woman who understands the scriptural values in marriage prays for the erotic attraction between him- or herself and his or her spouse to grow in depth and intensity over the years (Prov. 5:15-19; Eph. 5:33). A married person with possible cultural or personal value conflicts in this area may falsely expect the erotic attraction in his or her marriage to decrease over time and may begin to look for affection outside of the marriage relationship (Mal. 2:14-15; Eph. 5: 28-29).

## Expectancy and Gratitude Issues

• A person with solid biblical values in this area allows for and anticipates God's power to change the natural order of events on strategic occasions (Deut. 6:22-23; Acts 2:22). A person with possible cultural or personal conflicts in this area may not believe in a spiritual universe or divine intervention (Dan. 5: 2, 5-31; Acts 20: 28).

• A believer with biblical expectations in this area feels free to pray with a prayer partner for specific needs to be met (Mal. 1:9; 3:10; Matt. 18:18-20). Sadly, an individual with possible cultural or personal value conflicts in this area may not expect God to answer his or her prayer in any concrete way (2 Kings 3:10, 14-20; Matt. 27:41-43).

• An individual with a biblical value base in this area expresses frequent private and public gratitude to God and others when things go well (1 Chron. 16:29; Col. 2:6-7). A person with possible cultural or personal value conflicts in this area may find it difficult to give credit to God and/or other people and may instead give credit only to him- or herself (2 Kings 5:1-14; Matt. 18:18-23).

## Spiritual and Emotional Issues

• A person with solid biblical grounding knows what it means to initiate a personal relationship with God through Jesus Christ (Josh. 24:15; John 3:16). In comparison, an individual with possible cultural or personal value conflicts in this area may substitute self-worship, philosophy, science, or even religious tradition for a primary relationship with God (Ps. 14:1; Col. 2:8).

• An individual with biblical grounding in this area is led by the Holy Spirit through daily Bible reading and prayer (Ps. 39:12; 2 Tim. 3:15). An individual with possible cultural or personal value conflicts in this area may seldom or never read the Bible or pray for God's guidance (Matt. 22:29; Heb. 2:3).

• An individual with biblical values in this area develops his or her sense of acceptance and assurance by sharing thoughts and emotions with God the Father throughout the day (Ps. 42:8; 2 John 5:14). However, an individual with possible cultural or personal value conflicts in this area may be unsure of his or her right to pray and may feel negative about God's involvement in his or her life (Gen. 25:32; James 1:6-8).

• An individual with biblical awareness in this area allows God's love to heal past personal and emotional scars as they are uncovered through sharing with a concerned friend or counselor (Ps. 147:3; 2 John 1:3). An individual with possible cultural or personal value conflicts in this area tends to deny that self-acceptance or healing from despair has anything to do with God (Prov. 1:30-31; 2 Cor. 4:8).

• An individual who accepts scriptural principles in this area continually forgives him- or herself (by God's grace) and forgives others in order to maintain a close, warm, trusting relationship with the Father, Son, and Holy Spirit (James 5:16; 1 John 1:7-9). An individual with possible cultural or personal value conflicts in this area may fail to forgive him- or herself and/or others and may allow bitterness and resentment to block any sense of closeness and relationship with a caring God (Job 7:11; John 2:11).

## The Counselor's Journal

• As you develop as a committed counselor, you may find it useful and interesting to keep a confidential journal on the types of values and value conflicts people present to you. You may even wish to explore some basic statistical research in terms of the frequency of the particular kinds of situations that are brought to you for help.

# Topical Scripture References

## Love Scriptures

Emphasize the warmth of these Love Scriptures for ready reference by highlighting each one with a pink highlighter in your Bible.

### The Greatness of Love

I Corinthians 13:13
John 13:34
Romans 12:10
Colossians 3:14
Romans 5:8

### The Source of Love

2 Peter 1:4, 7
I John 3:1
I John 4:7
3 John 1:5-6
Ephesians 1:4

### The Qualities of Love

Galatians 5:13-14
Ephesians 4:32
I Corinthians 13:4
I Corinthians 13:7
Hebrews 13:1-2

### The Sacrifice of Love

John 3:16
John 14:23
John 15:12-13
I Timothy 1:5
I Peter 4:8-10

## Sex and Marriage Scriptures

Make these Sex and Marriage Scriptures easily available by highlighting each one with a blue highlighter in your Bible.

### Ideals for Marriage

I Corinthians 11:11
Ephesians 5:2
I Timothy 3:2
Titus 2:4-5
Ephesians 5:33

### Sexuality in Marriage

Mark 10:6-8
I Corinthians 7:2
I Corinthians 7:4
Ephesians 5:25
Ephesians 5:28

## Purity in Marriage
2 Timothy 2:22
Hebrews 13:4
1 Corinthians 7:5
Matthew 5:27-28
John 8:10-11

## Maturity in Marriage
Romans 13:13
1 Corinthians 7:10
1 Corinthians 7:27
Colossians 3:13
Colossians 3:16

## Faith Scriptures
Strengthen your ability to believe for and with your clients as you highlight each of these Faith Scriptures with a yellow highlighter in your Bible.

### The Foundation of Faith
John 3:17
Ephesians 2:4-5
Colossians 1:19-20
Colossians 1:27
1 John 3:3

### The Search of Faith
Luke 19:10
John 5:24
Romans 9:25-26
Hebrews 11:6
1 John 3:2

### The Challenge of Faith
Matthew 18:3
John 3:3
Acts 4:12
Romans 10:9
Ephesians 2:8

### The Future of Faith
2 Corinthians 8:9
Hebrews 11:1
Hebrews 11:8
Hebrews 13:8
1 John 5:4-5

## Success Scriptures
Anticipate the rewards of these Success Scriptures, for yourself and your clients, as you highlight each one with a green highlighter in your Bible.

### The Promise of Success
2 Corinthians 9:8
Ephesians 1:3
Hebrews 13:6
2 Timothy 1:7
Hebrews 6:15

### Preparation for Success
Acts 1:5
1 Corinthians 16:13
Galatians 6:7, 10
Hebrews 3:13-14
Hebrews 6:12

### The Increase of Success
Matthew 7:7-8
2 Corinthians 9:10
Philippians 4:17, 19
3 John 1:2
1 Timothy 6:6

### The Responsibility of Success
Matthew 6:33
Matthew 25:21
Romans 2:6-7
Hebrews 2:14-16
Colossians 3:2-3

## Miracle Scriptures

Allow the power of the Holy Spirit to confirm these Miracle Scriptures for you and your clients. Highlight each one with a lavender highlighter in your Bible.

### Healing Miracles of Jesus

Matthew 4:23
Matthew 8:3
Mark 2:3, 5
Luke 4:38-39
John 9:1, 7

### Miracles of Disciples

Matthew 10:1
Mark 16:15, 20
Acts 3:2, 8
Acts 12:5, 7
Acts 14:8, 10

### Deliverance Miracles of Jesus

Matthew 12:28
Matthew 17:15, 18
Mark 5:2, 13
Luke 9:42
Luke 13:11, 13, 16

### Miracles of the Redeemed

John 14:12-13
Romans 8:11
1 Corinthians 12:10
Hebrews 2:3-4
James 5:15-16

# Skill Builders Index

**Chapter 1**

1.1 Bishop's Wife **4**
1.2 Recovery Tool **6**
1.3 Girlfriend **8**
1.4 Trying to Cheat Me **10**
1.5 Vice President **12**
1.6 Under the Table **14**
1.7 Remarried **16**
1.8 Nightmares **18**
1.9 Not Very Married **20**
1.10 Can't Tell Mom **22**
1.11 Suicide **23**

**Chapter 2**

2.1 Counseling Opportunities **30**
2.2 Why Now? **32**
2.3 Emotion and Content **33**
2.4 Changing Gears **35**
2.5 Empathy Sandwich **37**
2.6 Give-and-Take Translation **40**
2.7 Ain't-It-Awful Lists **42**
2.8 Question Trap **44**
2.9 Deep Listening **46**

**Chapter 3**

3.1 Parrot Practice **59**
3.2 Listening to the Three Spirits **62**
3.3 Emotional Jigsaw Puzzle **64**
3.4 Facts and Feelings **67**
3.5 Beliefs and Feelings **70**
3.6 Possible Goals **73**

**Chapter 4**

4.1 Connecting Content and Emotion **81**
4.2 Connecting Emotion and Value **83**
4.3 Suggesting Options **85**
4.4 Listening for Causes **88**

**Chapter 5**

5.1 Prompts/Probes **97**
5.2 Sentence Probes **99**
5.3 Direct Requests **100**
5.4 Minimal Prompts **102**
5.5 Empathy/Probes **104**
5.6 Scripture/Probes **105**

**Chapter 6**

6.1 Goals and Activities **117**
6.2 Missing Data **119**
6.3 Brainstorming Invitations **122**
6.4 Hopes, Goals, and Commitments **123**
6.5 "Nick's Nine" Evaluation **125**
6.6 "C-R-A-V-E" Chart **127**
6.7 Timetables **129**
6.8 Six-Step Prayer **131**
6.9 Personal Action Plan **135**

**Chapter 7**

7.1 Spiritual Probe Questions 147
7.2 Reflection Statements 148
7.3 Transforming Perspectives 151
7.4 Emotions Scripture Passages 153
7.5 Scriptural Empathy Sandwiches
155
7.6 Scriptural Responses 158
7.7 Restating Decisions 160

**Chapter 8**

8.1 Prayer Experiences 169
8.2 Healing Experiences 172
8.3 Parents and God 174

8.4 Scripture and Christ 176
8.5 Counseling Probes 178
8.6 Private Prayer 180
8.7 Prayer Problems 181

**Chapter 9**

9.1 Demonic Experiences 190
9.2 Discussing Demons 192
9.3 Emotional Healing 194
9.4 Christian Authority 196
9.5 Counseling Parents 197
9.6 Responsibility and Authority 200
9.7 Self-Esteem 203
9.8 Healing Effectiveness 205

# Encouragement for Your Future

*San Diego may be one of the most beautiful cities in the United States, with its miles of beaches, warm climate, wonderful food, and a pervasive sense of newness and adventure, combined with antiquity and charm. San Diego has special meaning for me.*

*One of my greatest joys was to revisit San Diego and meet again with Mr. Atwood, a wealthy corporation president, and his gracious wife. As my wife, Judy, and I shared dessert with them on their LaJolla veranda looking out over the ocean, we enjoyed the view and reminisced about Christian friends and leaders the four of us knew in common.*

*Although we didn't need to discuss it during this lovely visit, I thought back twelve years before to the day when Mrs. Atwood invited me to lunch with her at the San Diego Yacht Club to discuss her desire to divorce her husband—because he was having increasing fits of rage at home, during a time of financial and vocational crises when they almost lost everything. In my mind and heart, I contrasted that despairing day with the wonderfully rebuilt lives and fortunes of this marvelous family.*

THE JOY OF BEING a faith-based personal counselor comes from being positioned by God at the right time and the right place to be his agent for these miracles of restoration.

As you continue to be led by the Spirit of God in your use of increasing counseling skills, you will find God placing you at these critical, miraculous points of transformation in other people's lives!

May God richly bless you, and others through you, as you provide "apples of gold in settings of silver" (Prov. 25:11) in your ministry of counseling!

Sincerely,

John R. Cheydleur, Ph.D., ACSW
West Nyack, New York
914-620-7383
Cheydleur@Juno.com

P.S. Add to your counseling skills and discover a wealth of Christian fellowship and support by joining one of these Christian professional organizations:

North American Association of Christians in Social Work
(888) 426-4712
www.nacsw.org

American Association of Christian Counselors
(800) 520-2268
www.aacc.net

Christian Association for Psychological Studies
(830) 629-2277
www.capsintl@compuvision.net

# Author Information

## JOHN R. CHEYDLEUR, PH.D., ACSW

Captain/Dr. John Cheydleur is a Salvation Army officer who serves as the Counseling Studies Coordinator at The School for Officer Training, Suffern, New York. In addition, as Eastern (U.S.A.) Territorial Social Services Secretary, Dr. Cheydleur provides consultation and policy oversight to a network of 2700 social service programs operated by The Salvation Army in eleven northeastern states and Puerto Rico.

Dr. Cheydleur is the author of the personality-development and spiritual-gifts book *How to Find and Be Yourself* and is the coeditor of the addictions self-help book *Every Sober Day Is a Miracle*. He is a contributor to *Baker's Encyclopedia of Psychology* and is the author of more than thirty other popular and professional articles and a mental-health television series.

He has also served as the president of the Personality Development Institute at Anaheim, California; president of Trinity College of Graduate Studies in Anaheim, California; chairman of the Department of Social Work at Melodyland School of Theology in Anaheim, California; director of The Salvation Army's San Diego County Bureau of Social Services; and U.S.-Canadian administrator of the Kiwanis International Collegiate Program: Circle K. International.

He is a member of the Christian Association for Psychological Studies, the American Association of Christian Counselors, the North American Association of Christians in Social Work, and the Academy of Certified Social Workers.

John, along with his wife, Judith, and their son Andrew, lives in West Nyack, New York. They also have two grown children, Amy and James, and five grandchildren.